sauces
100 everyday recipes

First published in 2012
LOVE FOOD is an imprint of Parragon Books Ltd

Parragon
Queen Street House
4 Queen Street
Bath BA1 1HE, UK

www.parragon.com

ISBN: 978-1-4454-6636-1

Printed in China

Produced by Ivy Contract
Cover photography by Mike Cooper
Cover image home economy and food styling by Lincoln Jefferson

Notes for the Reader

This book uses both metric and imperial measurements. Follow the same units of measurement throughout; do not mix metric and imperial. All spoon measurements are level: teaspoons are assumed to be 5 ml, and tablespoons are assumed to be 15 ml. Unless otherwise stated, milk is assumed to be full fat, eggs and individual vegetables are medium, and pepper is freshly ground black pepper.

The times given are an approximate guide only. Preparation times differ according to the techniques used by different people and the cooking times may also vary from those given. Optional ingredients, variations or serving suggestions have not been included in the calculations.

Recipes using raw or very lightly cooked eggs should be avoided by infants, the elderly, pregnant women, convalescents and anyone suffering from an illness. Pregnant and breastfeeding women are advised to avoid eating peanuts and peanut products. Sufferers from nut allergies should be aware that some of the ready-made ingredients used in the recipes in this book may contain nuts. Always check the packaging before use.

sauces

introduction   4

classics   6

pasta sauces   58

dressings   118

salsas   144

sweet sauces   182

index   208

introduction

Sauces are a cook's best friend. Deceptively easy to make, a home-made sauce looks impressive and adds a touch of finesse to any meal. A well-chosen sauce can really elevate a meal, providing a burst of intense flavour to complement subtler tastes, adding moistness to drier foods and giving a contrast of texture and colour to add depth to a dish.

And there's no reason a sauce has to be the supporting act: some of the fabulous sauces included in this book are really the star of the show, from the favourite Bolognese sauce – which can be paired with spaghetti to create the classic Italian dish, or provide base for a hearty cottage pie – to Tex-Mex salsa, which just needs a few tortilla chips to make a great sharing dish for friends.

The versatility of sauces means you can make a different meal every night, simply by mixing and matching the sauce to the food. Grilled chicken served with a satay sauce can transport your imagination to the palm fringed beaches of Thailand. Dress your grilled chicken with tapenade and you can taste Provence.

Many of the sauces in this book can be made in bulk and frozen for another occasion, and salad dressings and cold sauces can easily be bottled and transported for picnics and barbecues.

It's worth remembering that the recipes in this book can also be adjusted to suit your own preferences. Make a yogurt salsa lower in fat by using fat free yoghurt, or reduce the calories in your Béchamel sauce by using skimmed milk. Using a plain sauce as a base, you can add ingredients to make wholly new creations: add blue cheese to your Béchamel sauce to make a mouthwateringly indulgent blue cheese sauce, or mix mascarpone into your fresh tomato sauce to make a rich pasta sauce that is the basis of a quick but irresistible midweek meal.

So go ahead — experiment, and soon you'll have a trusted repertoire of sauces up your sleeve to turn any meal into something special. You'll have everyone begging to share your secrets!

classics

béchamel sauce

ingredients

makes about 350 ml/
12 fl oz

300 ml/10 fl oz milk
1 small onion, studded
    with 2–3 cloves
1 mace blade
1 fresh bay leaf
3–4 white or black peppercorns
1 small carrot, peeled
2 tbsp unsalted butter
    or margarine
35 g/1¼ oz plain flour
salt and pepper

method

1 Pour the milk into a small heavy-based saucepan with a lid. Add the onion, mace, bay leaf, peppercorns and carrot. Heat over a gentle heat and slowly bring to just boiling point. Remove from the heat, cover and set aside for at least 30 minutes. Strain and reheat until warm.

2 Melt the butter in a separate small saucepan and sprinkle in the flour. Cook over a gentle heat, stirring constantly with a wooden spoon, for 2 minutes.

3 Remove from the heat and gradually stir in the warmed infused milk, adding a little at a time and stirring until the milk has been incorporated before adding more. When all the milk has been added, return to the heat and cook, stirring, until thick, smooth and glossy. Add salt and pepper to taste and serve.

béarnaise sauce

ingredients

makes about 125 ml/
4 fl oz

4 tbsp tarragon vinegar
1 shallot, finely chopped
2 egg yolks
85 g/3 oz unsalted butter, softened
salt and pepper

method

1 Put the vinegar and shallot in a small heavy-based saucepan over a medium–low heat and let simmer until reduced to 1 tablespoon. Leave to cool.

2 Strain the vinegar mixture into a heatproof bowl and set over a pan of simmering water. Add the egg yolks and mix together until thick. Gradually add the butter in small pieces, whisking after each addition, until combined and the sauce has thickened. Season to taste with salt and pepper and serve.

hollandaise sauce

ingredients

makes about 175 ml/
6 fl oz

2 tbsp white wine vinegar
1 tbsp water
2 egg yolks
115 g/4 oz unsalted butter,
    slightly softened and diced
lemon juice (optional)
salt and pepper

method

1 Pour the vinegar and water into a small heavy-based saucepan and bring to the boil. Boil for 3 minutes, or until reduced by half. Remove from the heat and leave to cool slightly.

2 Put the egg yolks in a heatproof bowl and beat in the cooled vinegar water. Set over a saucepan of gently simmering water, ensuring that the base of the bowl does not touch the simmering water.

3 Cook, stirring constantly with a wooden spoon, until the mixture thickens slightly and lightly coats the back of the spoon.

4 Keeping the water simmering, add the butter, a piece at a time, stirring until the sauce is thick, smooth and glossy. Add a little lemon juice if the mixture is too thick and to give a more piquant flavour. Add salt and pepper to taste and serve warm.

velouté sauce

ingredients

*makes about 350 ml/
12 fl oz*

25 g/1 oz unsalted butter
2 tbsp plain flour
350 ml/12 fl oz chicken stock,
    warmed
2–3 tbsp single cream
1–2 tbsp freshly squeezed
    lemon juice
salt and pepper
grilled chicken and French beans,
    to serve

method

1 Heat the butter in a small heavy-based saucepan until melted, then sprinkle in the flour. Cook over a gentle heat, stirring constantly with a wooden spoon, for 2 minutes.

2 Remove from the heat and gradually stir in the warmed stock, stirring thoroughly after each addition. When all the stock has been added, return to the heat and cook, stirring constantly, until the sauce is reduced slightly, has thickened and lightly coats the back of the spoon.

3 Remove from the heat and stir in the cream with the lemon juice and salt and pepper to taste. Serve warm with grilled chicken and French beans.

beurre blanc

ingredients

makes about 125ml/
4 fl oz

2 tbsp finely chopped shallot
2 tbsp white wine vinegar
115 g/4 oz unsalted butter
salt and pepper
steamed fish and vegetables,
    to serve

method

1 Put the shallot in a small heavy-based saucepan with the vinegar and salt and pepper to taste. Bring to the boil and boil for 2–3 minutes until reduced to about 2 teaspoons.

2 Add 25 g/1 oz of the butter and beat vigorously with a wire whisk while bringing to the boil. Remove from the heat and whisk in the remaining butter, a piece at a time. When all the butter has been added, check and adjust the seasoning if necessary, and serve with steamed fish and vegetables.

bread sauce

ingredients

makes about 600 ml/
1 pint

1 onion
12 cloves
1 bay leaf
6 black peppercorns
600 ml/1 pint milk
115 g/4 oz fresh white
    breadcrumbs
2 tbsp butter
whole nutmeg, for grating
2 tbsp double cream (optional)
salt and pepper

method

1 Make small holes in the onion using the point of a
sharp knife or a skewer, and push the cloves in them.

2 Put the onion, bay leaf and peppercorns in a saucepan
and pour in the milk. Bring to the boil, then remove
from the heat, cover and leave to infuse for 1 hour.

3 To make the sauce, discard the onion and bay leaf and
strain the milk to remove the peppercorns. Return the
milk to the cleaned pan and add the breadcrumbs.

4 Cook the sauce over a very low heat for 4–5 minutes,
until the breadcrumbs have swollen and the sauce
is thick.

5 Beat in the butter and season well with salt and
pepper and a good grating of nutmeg. Stir in the
cream just before serving, if using.

parsley sauce

ingredients

*makes about 300 ml/
10 fl oz*

2–3 sprigs fresh parsley
25 g/1 oz butter, melted
25 g/1 oz plain flour
300 ml/10 fl oz milk
pinch of freshly grated nutmeg
salt and pepper

method

1 Bring a small saucepan of water to the boil and blanch the parsley sprigs for 30 seconds. Drain, refresh under cold water, then strip off the leaves and chop finely.

2 Put the butter, flour and milk into a food processor and process until smooth. Pour into a saucepan and bring to the boil over a low heat, stirring constantly. Continue to boil, stirring constantly, for 3–4 minutes until thickened and smooth.

3 Remove from the heat, stir in the parsley and season to taste with nutmeg and salt and pepper before serving.

asparagus sauce

ingredients

makes about 300 ml/
10 fl oz

150 ml/5 fl oz chicken stock
1 bouquet garni, consisting of
    3 fresh parsley sprigs, 2 fresh
    thyme sprigs, 1 bay leaf and a
    small celery stick tied together
2 mushrooms, chopped
6 spring onions, chopped
700 g/1 lb 9 oz green asparagus
40 g/1½ oz butter
4 tbsp chopped fresh parsley
2 tbsp plain flour
1 tbsp caster sugar
salt and pepper

method

1 Put the chicken stock into a saucepan and add the bouquet garni, mushrooms and 2 of the spring onions. Bring to the boil, then reduce the heat, cover and simmer gently for 20 minutes.

2 Meanwhile, cut off and discard the woody ends of the asparagus stems. Blanch in lightly salted boiling water for 2 minutes, then drain and refresh under cold water. Drain well again.

3 Melt 25 g/1 oz of the butter in a heavy-based frying pan over a medium heat. Add the asparagus, parsley and remaining spring onions and cook, stirring gently, for 5 minutes. Remove from the heat. Using a fork, mash the remaining butter with the flour to a paste to make beurre manié. Remove and discard the bouquet garni from the chicken stock. Gradually stir in small pieces of the beurre manié until they are absorbed and the mixture is thickened. Remove from the heat and leave to cool slightly.

4 Transfer the asparagus mixture to a blender and add the sugar and 4 tablespoons of the stock mixture. Season with salt and pepper. Process to a smooth purée, adding stock mixture until you achieve the desired consistency. Taste and adjust the seasoning before serving.

mild horseradish sauce

ingredients

makes about 175 ml/
6 fl oz

6 tbsp creamed horseradish sauce
6 tbsp crème fraîche

method

1 In a small serving bowl, mix the horseradish sauce and crème fraîche together.

2 Serve the sauce with roast beef, or with smoked fish such as trout or mackerel.

mint sauce

ingredients

makes about 125 ml/
4 fl oz

3 tbsp chopped fresh mint

2–3 tsp caster sugar, or to taste

2 tbsp just-boiled water

3–4 tbsp white wine vinegar
    or malt vinegar

method

1 Put the mint in a small heatproof bowl and add 2 teaspoons of the sugar. Allow the boiled water to cool for about 1 minute, then pour over the mint. Stir until the sugar has dissolved, then leave to infuse for 10 minutes.

2 Add the vinegar to taste, cover and leave to stand for 1 hour. Stir and serve.

basil pesto

ingredients

makes about 225 ml/
8 fl oz

55 g/2 oz fresh basil leaves
1 garlic clove
25 g/1 oz toasted pine kernels
125–150 ml/4–5 fl oz
    extra virgin olive oil
25 g/1 oz freshly grated
    Parmesan cheese
1–2 tsp freshly squeezed lemon
    juice (optional)
salt and pepper

method

1 Tear the basil leaves and put in a large mortar with the garlic, pine kernels and 1 tablespoon of the oil. Pound with a pestle to form a paste.

2 Gradually work in the remaining oil to form a thick sauce. Add salt and pepper to taste and stir in the Parmesan cheese. If liked, slacken slightly with the lemon juice.

sun-dried tomato pesto

ingredients

makes about 350 ml/
12 fl oz

25 g/1 oz pine kernels

2 garlic cloves, coarsely chopped

225 g/8 oz sun-dried tomatoes
   in oil, drained and coarsely
   chopped

1 tsp coarse salt

25 g/1 oz freshly grated
   Parmesan cheese

125–150 ml/4–5 fl oz
   extra virgin olive oil

method

1 Dry-fry the pine kernels in a heavy-based frying pan for
   30–60 seconds until golden. Remove from the pan
   and leave to cool.

2 Place in the food processor with the garlic, sun-dried
   tomatoes and salt. Process to a purée. Add the
   Parmesan cheese and process briefly again. Then
   add 125 ml/4 fl oz of the oil and process again. If the
   consistency is too thick, add the remaining oil and
   process again until smooth.

tapenade

ingredients

makes about 400 ml/
14 fl oz

225 g/8 oz stoned black olives
40 g/1½ oz capers, drained
1 tbsp chopped fresh thyme
2 garlic cloves
1 tsp Dijon mustard
55 g/2 oz canned anchovy fillets
150 ml/5 fl oz virgin olive oil
about 2 tbsp brandy
1 tbsp chopped fresh
    flat-leaf parsley
pepper
grilled swordfish or tuna and
    French beans, to serve

method

1 Put the olives, capers, thyme, garlic and mustard
   in a food processor and process for 1 minute. Add
   the anchovy fillets with their oil and process for an
   additional 2–3 minutes until a thick paste is formed.

2 With the motor running, slowly pour in the oil in a thin,
   steady stream until a thick sauce is formed.

3 Scrape into a bowl and stir in enough brandy to give a
   thick sauce. Add pepper to taste and stir in the parsley.
   Spoon into a small serving bowl and serve with grilled
   swordfish or tuna and French beans.

apple sauce

ingredients

*makes about 450 ml/
16 fl oz*

about 5 large tart cooking apples,
    about 900 g/2 lb total weight
85 g/3 oz caster sugar
2–3 tbsp water
25 g/1 oz unsalted butter

method

1 Peel, core and chop the apples. Place in a heavy-based saucepan with the sugar and water. Bring to the boil, then reduce the heat, cover and simmer, stirring occasionally, for 10–12 minutes, or until the apples have collapsed and are fluffy.

2 Add the butter and stir until melted. Beat with a wooden spoon until smooth. Serve warm or cold.

variation

Boil the apples, sugar and water with the grated rind of ½ lemon and 1 cinnamon stick to give the sauce extra flavour.

cranberry sauce

ingredients

makes about 450 ml/
16 fl oz

450 g/1 lb fresh or thawed
frozen cranberries
1 tbsp grated orange rind,
preferably unwaxed
150 ml/5 fl oz freshly squeezed
orange juice
115 g/4 oz soft light brown sugar
150 ml/5 fl oz water
1–2 tbsp Cointreau (optional)

method

1 Put the cranberries in a heavy-based saucepan with the orange rind and juice, most of the sugar and the water. Bring to the boil, then reduce the heat and simmer for 12–15 minutes until the cranberries have burst.

2 Remove from the heat, taste and add the remaining sugar, if liked, with the Cointreau, if using. Serve warm or cold.

gravy

ingredients

makes about 1.2 litres/
2 pints

900 g/2 lb meat bones,
    raw or cooked
1 large onion, chopped
1 large carrot, chopped
2 celery sticks, chopped
1 bouquet garni
1.7 litres/3 pints water

method

1 Preheat the oven to 200°C/400°F/Gas Mark 6. Put the bones in a roasting tin and roast in the preheated oven for 20 minutes, or until browned. Remove from the oven and leave to cool.

2 Chop the bones into small pieces and put in a large saucepan with all the remaining ingredients. Bring to the boil, then reduce the heat, cover and simmer for 2 hours.

3 Strain and leave until cold, then remove all traces of fat. Store, covered, in the refrigerator for up to 4 days. Boil vigorously for 5 minutes before using. The gravy can be frozen in ice-cube trays for up to 1 month.

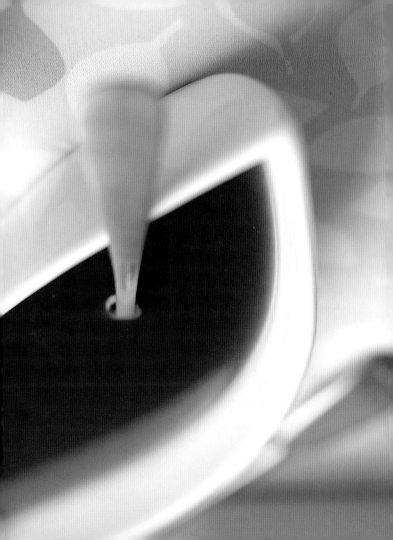

red wine sauce

ingredients

*makes about 225 ml/
8 fl oz*

150 ml/5 fl oz gravy
4 tbsp red wine, such as
    a Burgundy
1 tbsp redcurrant jelly

method

1 Blend the gravy with the wine and pour into a small
   heavy-based saucepan. Add the redcurrant jelly and
   warm over a gentle heat, stirring, until blended.

2 Bring to the boil, then reduce the heat and simmer
   for 2 minutes. Serve hot.

teriyaki sauce

ingredients

*makes about 225 ml/
8 fl oz*

2.5-cm/1-inch piece fresh ginger
300 ml/10 fl oz shoyu
    (Japanese soy sauce)
3 tbsp white wine vinegar or
    cider vinegar
3 tbsp mirin (sweet rice wine)
2–3 tbsp caster sugar

method

1 Peel and grate the ginger. Put the ginger in a small heavy-based saucepan with the shoyu, vinegar, mirin and 2 tablespoons of the sugar.

2 Gently heat, stirring, until the sugar has dissolved. Taste and add the remaining sugar, if liked.

3 Boil the mixture for 5–8 minutes, or until reduced by half. Remove from the heat. If you want to use it immediately, stand the sauce in a bowl of ice and water for 30 minutes, or until cool. Alternatively, leave until cool, then use as required.

satay sauce

ingredients

makes about 225 ml/
8 fl oz

4 spring onions, coarsely chopped
1 garlic clove, coarsely chopped
2 tsp chopped fresh ginger
6 tbsp peanut butter
1 tsp muscovado sugar
1 tsp Thai fish sauce
2 tbsp soy sauce
1 tbsp chilli sauce or a few
    drops of Tabasco sauce
1 tsp lemon juice
salt
peanuts, to garnish

method

1 Put all the ingredients into a food processor.
   Add 150 ml/5 fl oz water and process to a purée.

2 Transfer to a saucepan, season to taste with salt and
   heat gently, stirring occasionally. Transfer to a bowl
   and sprinkle with the peanuts. Serve warm or cold.

sweet & sour sauce

ingredients

*makes about 225 ml/
8 fl oz*

3 tbsp white rice vinegar
2 tbsp sugar
1 tbsp light soy sauce
1 tbsp tomato ketchup
1½ tbsp vegetable or
    groundnut oil
1 green pepper, roughly chopped
1 small onion, roughly chopped
1 small carrot, finely sliced
½ tsp finely chopped garlic
½ tsp finely chopped fresh ginger
100 g/3½ oz pineapple chunks
stir-fried meat, to serve

method

1 Mix the vinegar, sugar, soy sauce and ketchup together.
   Set aside.

2 In a preheated wok or deep saucepan, heat
   1 tablespoon of the oil and stir-fry the green pepper,
   onion and carrot for 2 minutes. Remove and set aside.

3 Clean out the wok, heat the remaining oil and stir-fry
   the garlic and ginger until fragrant. Add the vinegar
   mixture. Bring back to the boil and add the pineapple
   chunks. Finally add the pepper, onion and carrot. Stir
   until warmed through and serve immediately with
   stir-fried meat of your choice.

chilli sauce

ingredients

*makes about 450 ml/
16 fl oz*

5 large fresh mild chillies
450 ml/16 fl oz hot vegetable
    stock
1 tbsp masa harina or 1 crumbled
    corn tortilla, puréed with
    enough water to make
    a thin paste
large pinch of ground cumin
1–2 garlic cloves, finely chopped
juice of 1 lime
salt

method

1 Preheat the grill to high. Using metal tongs, roast each chilli under a hot grill until the colour darkens on all sides. Put the chillies in a bowl and pour boiling water over them. Cover and leave to cool. When the chillies have cooled and are swollen and soft, remove from the water with a slotted spoon. Deseed, then cut the flesh into pieces and place in a food processor. Process to a purée, then mix in the hot stock.

2 Put the chilli and stock mixture in a saucepan. Add the masa harina, cumin, garlic and lime juice. Bring to the boil and cook for a few minutes, stirring, until the sauce has thickened. Adjust the seasoning and serve.

mole sauce

ingredients

makes about 850ml/
1½ pints

9 mixed chillies, soaked in
    hot water for 30 minutes
    and drained
1 onion, sliced
2–3 garlic cloves, crushed
85 g/3 oz sesame seeds
85 g/3 oz toasted flaked almonds
1 tsp ground coriander
4 cloves
½ tsp pepper
2–3 tbsp sunflower oil
300 ml/10 fl oz chicken
    or vegetable stock
450 g/1 lb ripe tomatoes,
    peeled and chopped
2 tsp ground cinnamon
55 g/2 oz raisins
140 g/5 oz pumpkin seeds
55 g/2 oz plain chocolate,
    broken into pieces
1 tbsp red wine vinegar

method

1 Put the chillies in a food processor with the onion,
   garlic, sesame seeds, almonds, coriander, cloves and
   pepper and process to form a thick paste.

2 Heat the oil in a saucepan, add the paste, and fry for
   5 minutes. Add the stock with the tomatoes, cinnamon,
   raisins and pumpkin seeds. Bring to the boil, reduce the
   heat and simmer, stirring occasionally, for 15 minutes.

3 Add the chocolate and vinegar to the sauce. Cook
   gently for 5 minutes, then use as required.

chipotle sauce

ingredients

*makes about 600 ml/
1 pint*

2–4 dried chipotle chillies
2 tbsp olive oil
4 streaky bacon rashers, chopped
1 large onion, finely chopped
2–3 garlic cloves, crushed
2 celery sticks, finely chopped
2 tbsp tomato purée
150 ml/5 fl oz stout,
    such as Guinness
150 ml/5 fl oz vegetable
    or brown stock
2 tbsp dark muscovado sugar
1 tsp prepared English mustard
1–2 tsp Worcestershire sauce
2 tbsp chopped fresh coriander
pepper
beefburgers and salad, to serve

method

1 Put the chillies in a heatproof bowl, pour over hot water to cover and soak for 30 minutes, or until softened. Drain, reserving the soaking liquid, and finely chop the chillies.

2 Heat the oil in a heavy-based saucepan, add the bacon, onion, garlic and celery, and sauté, stirring frequently, for 15 minutes. Blend the tomato purée with the reserved soaking liquid and stir into the saucepan, then add the chillies, stout and stock. Add the sugar with the mustard and Worcestershire sauce, stir well and bring to the boil.

3 Reduce the heat, cover and simmer, stirring occasionally, for 30 minutes. Add pepper to taste and stir in the coriander. Serve with beefburgers and salad.

barbecue sauce

ingredients

*makes about 225 ml/
8 fl oz*

1 tbsp olive oil
1 small onion, finely chopped
2–3 garlic cloves, crushed
1 fresh red jalapeño chilli,
    deseeded and finely chopped
    (optional)
2 tsp tomato purée
1 tsp (or to taste) dry mustard
1 tbsp red wine vinegar
1 tbsp Worcestershire sauce
2–3 tsp muscovado sugar
300 ml/10 fl oz water

method

1 Heat the oil in a small heavy-based saucepan, add the onion, garlic and chilli, if using, and gently sauté, stirring frequently, for 3 minutes, or until beginning to soften. Remove from the heat.

2 Blend the tomato purée with the mustard, vinegar and Worcestershire sauce to form a paste, then stir into the onion mixture with 2 teaspoons of the sugar. Mix well, then gradually stir in the water.

3 Return to the heat and bring to the boil, stirring frequently. Reduce the heat and gently simmer, stirring occasionally, for 15 minutes. Taste and add the remaining sugar, if liked. Strain, if preferred, and serve hot or leave to cool and serve cold.

fresh tomato sauce

ingredients

makes about 600 ml/
1 pint

1 tbsp olive oil
1 small onion, chopped
2–3 garlic cloves, crushed
    (optional)
1 small celery stick, finely chopped
1 bay leaf
450 g/1 lb ripe tomatoes, peeled
    and chopped
1 tbsp tomato purée, blended
    with 150 ml/5 fl oz water
few sprigs fresh oregano
pepper

method

1 Heat the oil in a heavy-based saucepan, add the onion,
garlic, if using, celery and bay leaf, and gently sauté,
stirring frequently, for 5 minutes.

2 Stir in the tomatoes with the blended tomato purée.
Add pepper to taste and the oregano. Bring to the
boil, then reduce the heat, cover and simmer, stirring
occasionally, for 20–25 minutes until the tomatoes
have completely collapsed. If liked, simmer for a further
20 minutes to give a thicker sauce.

3 Discard the bay leaf and the oregano. Transfer to a food
processor and process to a chunky purée. If a smooth
sauce is preferred, pass through a fine non-metallic
sieve. Taste and adjust the seasoning if necessary.
Reheat and use as required.

pasta sauces

arrabbiata sauce

ingredients

makes about 600 ml/
1 pint

2 tbsp olive oil
2 garlic cloves, chopped
1 fresh red serrano chilli,
    deseeded and chopped
1 tbsp grated lemon rind
450 g/1 lb ripe tomatoes,
    peeled and chopped
1 tbsp tomato purée, blended
    with 150 ml/5 fl oz water
pinch of caster sugar
1 tbsp balsamic vinegar
1 tbsp chopped fresh marjoram
pepper

method

1 Heat the oil in a heavy-based saucepan, add the garlic
    and chilli and sauté, stirring constantly, for 1 minute.
    Sprinkle in the lemon rind and stir, then add the
    tomatoes with the blended tomato purée. Add the
    sugar and bring to the boil, then reduce the heat
    and simmer for 12 minutes.

2 Add the vinegar and marjoram and simmer for a
    further 5 minutes. Add pepper to taste. Serve hot.

sun-dried tomato sauce

ingredients

serves 4

500 g/1 lb 2 oz minced lean beef
55 g/2 oz soft white breadcrumbs
1 garlic clove, crushed
2 tbsp chopped fresh parsley
1 tsp dried oregano
pinch of freshly grated nutmeg
¼ tsp ground coriander
55 g/2 oz freshly grated
   Parmesan cheese
2–3 tbsp milk
plain flour, for dusting
3 tbsp olive oil
400 g/14 oz dried tagliatelle
2 tbsp butter, diced

sauce

3 tbsp olive oil
2 large onions, sliced
2 celery sticks, thinly sliced
2 garlic cloves, chopped
400 g/14 oz canned chopped
   tomatoes
125 g/4½ oz sun-dried tomatoes
   in oil, drained and chopped
2 tbsp tomato purée
1 tbsp dark muscovado sugar
about 150 ml/5 fl oz white wine
salt and pepper

method

1 To make the sauce, heat the oil in a frying pan. Add the onions and celery and cook until translucent. Add the garlic and cook for 1 minute. Stir in all the tomatoes, tomato purée, sugar and wine and season to taste with salt and pepper. Bring to the boil and simmer for 10 minutes.

2 Meanwhile, break up the meat in a bowl with a wooden spoon until it becomes a sticky paste. Stir in the breadcrumbs, garlic, herbs and spices. Stir in the cheese and enough milk to make a firm paste. Flour your hands, take large spoonfuls of the mixture and shape it into 12 balls. Heat the oil in a frying pan and cook the meatballs for 5–6 minutes, or until browned.

3 Pour the tomato sauce over the meatballs. Lower the heat, cover the pan and simmer for 30 minutes, turning once or twice. Add a little extra wine if the sauce is beginning to become dry.

4 To cook the pasta, bring a large saucepan of lightly salted water to the boil. Add the pasta, bring back to the boil and cook for 8–10 minutes, or until tender but still firm to the bite. Drain, turn into a warmed serving dish, dot with the butter and toss with 2 forks. Spoon the meatballs and tomato sauce over the pasta and serve immediately.

mediterranean sauce

ingredients

serves 4

350 g/12 oz dried wholewheat
    spaghetti
1 tbsp olive oil
2 tbsp butter
sprigs of fresh basil, to garnish
crusty bread, to serve

sauce

1 tbsp olive oil
1 large red onion, chopped
2 garlic cloves, finely chopped
1 tbsp lemon juice
4 baby aubergines, cut into
    quarters
600 ml/1 pint passata
2 tsp caster sugar
2 tbsp tomato purée
400 g/14 oz canned artichoke
    hearts, drained and halved
115 g/4 oz black olives, stoned
salt and pepper

method

1 To make the sauce, heat the oil in a large frying pan.
Add the onion, garlic, lemon juice and aubergines and
cook over a low heat for 4–5 minutes, or until the onion
and aubergines become lightly golden.

2 Pour in the passata, season to taste with salt and black
pepper, and stir in the caster sugar and tomato purée.
Bring to the boil, then lower the heat and simmer,
stirring occasionally, for 20 minutes. Gently stir in
the artichoke hearts and black olives and cook for
5 minutes.

3 Meanwhile, to cook the pasta, bring a large saucepan
of lightly salted water to the boil. Add the spaghetti
and oil, bring back to the boil and cook for 8–12
minutes, or until tender but still firm to the bite.

4 Drain the spaghetti and toss with the butter. Transfer
to a large serving dish.

5 Pour the vegetable sauce over the spaghetti and
garnish with sprigs of fresh basil. Serve immediately
with crusty bread.

bolognese sauce

ingredients

serves 4

450 g/1 lb dried spaghetti
1 tbsp olive oil

sauce

2 tbsp olive oil
2 garlic cloves, crushed
1 large onion, finely chopped
1 carrot, diced
225 g/8 oz lean minced beef,
    veal or chicken
85 g/3 oz chicken livers,
    finely chopped
100 g/3½ oz lean Parma ham,
    diced
150 ml/5 fl oz Marsala
280 g/10 oz canned chopped
    plum tomatoes
1 tbsp chopped fresh basil leaves
2 tbsp tomato purée
salt and pepper

method

1 To make the sauce, heat the olive oil in a large saucepan. Add the garlic, onion and carrot and cook for 6 minutes.

2 Add the minced meat, chicken livers and Parma ham. Cook over a medium heat for 12 minutes, or until well browned.

3 Stir in the Marsala, tomatoes, basil and tomato purée and cook, stirring, for 4 minutes. Season to taste. Cover the pan and simmer for 30 minutes. Remove the lid, stir and simmer for a further 15 minutes.

4 Meanwhile, to cook the pasta, bring a large saucepan of lightly salted water to the boil. Add the spaghetti and oil, bring back to the boil and cook for 8–10 minutes, or until tender but still firm to the bite. Drain and transfer to a serving dish. Pour over the sauce and serve.

tarragon meatball sauce

ingredients

serves 4

450 g/1 lb fresh spaghetti

meatballs

150 g/5½ oz brown breadcrumbs
150 ml/5 fl oz milk
1 large onion, chopped
450 g/1 lb minced steak
1 tsp paprika
salt and pepper

sauce

2 tbsp butter
3 tbsp wholemeal flour
200 ml/7 fl oz beef stock
400 g/14 oz canned chopped
   tomatoes
2 tbsp tomato purée
1 tsp sugar
1 tbsp chopped fresh tarragon
4 tbsp olive oil
salt and pepper

method

1 Place the brown breadcrumbs in a bowl, add the milk and set aside to soak for 30 minutes.

2 To make the sauce, melt half of the butter in a saucepan. Add the flour and cook, stirring constantly, for 2 minutes. Gradually add the stock and cook, stirring constantly, for a further 5 minutes. Add the tomatoes, tomato purée, sugar and tarragon, reserving a little to garnish. Season well and simmer for 25 minutes.

3 Meanwhile, preheat the oven to 180°C/350°F/ Gas Mark 4. Mix the onion, minced steak and paprika into the breadcrumbs, and season to taste. Shape the mixture into 16 meatballs. Heat the oil and remaining butter in a frying pan and cook the meatballs, turning, until brown all over. Place in a casserole, pour over the tomato sauce, cover and bake in the preheated oven for 25 minutes.

4 To cook the pasta, bring a large saucepan of lightly salted water to the boil. Add the fresh spaghetti, bring back to the boil and cook for about 2–3 minutes, or until tender but still firm to the bite.

5 Remove the meatballs from the oven. Serve the meatballs and their sauce with the spaghetti, garnished with the reserved tarragon.

bucatini with lamb & yellow pepper sauce

ingredients

serves 4

250 g/9 oz dried bucatini

sauce
4 tbsp olive oil
280 g/10 oz boneless lamb, cubed
1 garlic clove, finely chopped
1 bay leaf
225 ml/8 fl oz dry white wine
2 large yellow peppers, deseeded and diced
4 tomatoes, peeled and chopped
salt and pepper

method

1 Heat half the olive oil in a large, heavy-based frying pan. Add the cubes of lamb and cook over a medium heat, stirring frequently, until browned on all sides. Add the garlic and cook for a further 1 minute. Add the bay leaf, pour in the wine and season to taste with salt and pepper. Bring to the boil and cook for 5 minutes, or until reduced.

2 Stir in the remaining oil, peppers and tomatoes. Reduce the heat, cover and simmer, stirring occasionally, for 45 minutes.

3 Meanwhile, bring a large, heavy-based saucepan of lightly salted water to the boil. Add the pasta, return to the boil and cook for 8–10 minutes, or until tender but still firm to the bite. Drain and transfer to a warmed serving dish. Remove and discard the bay leaf from the lamb sauce and spoon the sauce onto the pasta. Toss well together and serve immediately.

tomato, mushroom & bacon sauce

ingredients

serves 2

1 tbsp olive oil
1 small onion, finely chopped
1–2 garlic cloves, crushed
350 g/12 oz tomatoes,
    peeled and chopped
2 tsp tomato purée
2 tbsp water
300–350 g/10½–12 oz dried
    pasta shapes
90 g/3¼ oz lean rindless
    bacon, diced
40 g/1½ oz mushrooms, sliced
1 tbsp chopped fresh parsley
    or 1 tsp chopped fresh
    coriander
2 tbsp soured cream or natural
    fromage frais (optional)
salt and pepper

method

1 Heat the olive oil in a saucepan and fry the onion
   and garlic gently over a low heat until soft. Add the
   tomatoes, tomato purée and water to the mixture in
   the pan, season with salt and pepper to taste and bring
   to the boil. Cover and simmer gently for 10 minutes.

2 Meanwhile, cook the pasta in a large saucepan
   of boiling salted water for 8–10 minutes, or until
   tender but still firm to the bite.

3 Heat the bacon gently in a frying pan until the fat
   runs, add the mushrooms, and continue cooking for
   3–4 minutes. Drain off any excess fat.

4 Add the bacon and mushrooms to the tomato mixture,
   together with the parsley and the soured cream, if
   using, and reheat. Drain the pasta thoroughly and
   then transfer to warmed serving dishes. Stir through
   the sauce and serve immediately.

carbonara sauce

ingredients

serves 4

425 g/15 oz dried spaghetti
sprigs of fresh sage, to garnish
freshly grated Parmesan cheese,
    to serve (optional)

sauce

1 tbsp olive oil
1 large onion, thinly sliced
2 garlic cloves, chopped
175 g/6 oz rindless bacon,
    cut into thin strips
2 tbsp butter
175 g/6 oz mushrooms, sliced
300 ml/10 fl oz double cream
3 eggs, beaten
100 g/3½ oz Parmesan cheese,
    freshly grated
salt and pepper

method

1 Warm a large serving dish or bowl. To cook the pasta, bring a large saucepan of lightly salted water to the boil. Add the spaghetti, bring back to the boil and cook for 8–10 minutes, or until tender but still firm to the bite. Drain well, return to the pan and keep warm.

2 Meanwhile, to make the sauce, heat the olive oil in a frying pan over a medium heat. Add the onion and cook, stirring occasionally, for 2–3 minutes, or until translucent. Add the garlic and bacon and cook until the bacon is crisp. Transfer to the warm dish or bowl.

3 Melt the butter in the pan. Add the mushrooms and cook over a medium heat, stirring occasionally, for 3–4 minutes, or until tender. Return the bacon mixture to the pan. Cover and keep warm.

4 Combine the cream, eggs and cheese in a large bowl and season to taste. Working very quickly, tip the spaghetti into the bacon mixture and pour over the eggs. Toss the spaghetti quickly into the egg and cream mixture, using 2 forks. Garnish with sage and serve immediately with Parmesan cheese, if using.

variation

To offset the richness of the carbonara add the juice of ½ lemon or 60 ml/2 fl oz white wine to the dish.

pumpkin sauce with parma ham

ingredients

serves 4

250 g/9 oz dried green or
    white tagliatelle
1 tbsp olive oil
freshly grated Parmesan cheese,
    to serve

sauce

500 g/1 lb 2 oz pumpkin or
    butternut squash, peeled
2 tbsp olive oil
1 onion, finely chopped
2 garlic cloves, crushed
4–6 tbsp chopped fresh parsley
pinch of freshly grated nutmeg
about 300 ml/10 fl oz chicken
    stock or vegetable stock
115 g/4 oz Parma ham,
    cut into small pieces
150 ml/5 fl oz double cream
salt and pepper

method

1 To make the sauce, cut the pumpkin in half and scoop
   out the seeds with a spoon. Cut the pumpkin into
   1-cm/½-inch dice.

2 Heat the olive oil in a large saucepan. Add the onion
   and garlic and cook over a low heat for 3 minutes, or
   until soft. Add half the chopped parsley and cook for
   1 minute.

3 Add the pumpkin pieces and cook for 2–3 minutes.
   Season to taste with nutmeg, and salt and pepper.
   Add half the stock to the pan, bring to the boil, cover
   and simmer for about 10 minutes, or until the pumpkin
   is tender but still firm to the bite. Add more stock
   whenever the pumpkin is becoming dry and looks as
   if it might be about to burn. Add the Parma ham to
   the pan and cook, stirring, for a further 2 minutes.

4 Meanwhile, to cook the pasta, bring a large saucepan
   of lightly salted water to the boil. Add the tagliatelle
   and olive oil, bring back to the boil and cook for 8–10
   minutes, or until tender but still firm to the bite. Drain
   the pasta and transfer to a warmed serving dish. Stir
   the cream into the pumpkin and ham sauce and heat
   through well. Spoon the mixture over the tagliatelle.
   Sprinkle over the remaining parsley to garnish and
   serve immediately with Parmesan cheese.

creamy chicken sauce

ingredients

serves 4

1 quantity fresh tomato sauce
    (see page 56)
225 g/8 oz dried green tagliatelle
fresh basil leaves, to garnish

sauce

4 tbsp unsalted butter
400 g/14 oz skinless, boneless
    chicken breast portions,
    thinly sliced
85 g/3 oz blanched almonds
300 ml/10 fl oz double cream
salt and pepper

method

1 Make the tomato sauce, set aside and keep warm.
    To make the chicken sauce, melt the butter in a large,
    heavy frying pan over a medium heat. Add the
    chicken pieces and almonds and cook, stirring
    frequently, for about 5–6 minutes, or until the chicken
    is cooked through.

2 Meanwhile, pour the cream into a small saucepan, set
    over a low heat and bring to the boil. Continue to boil
    for 10 minutes, or until reduced by almost half. Pour
    the cream over the chicken and almonds, stir well and
    season with salt and pepper to taste. Remove the pan
    from the heat, set aside and keep warm.

3 To cook the pasta, bring a large saucepan of lightly
    salted water to the boil. Add the pasta, bring back to
    the boil and cook for 8–10 minutes, until tender but
    still firm to the bite. Drain the pasta, return to the pan,
    cover and keep warm until ready to serve.

4 When ready to serve, turn the pasta into a warmed
    serving dish and spoon the tomato sauce over it.
    Spoon the chicken and cream sauce into the centre,
    sprinkle with the basil leaves and serve.

seafood sauce

ingredients

serves 4

350 g/12 oz dried pasta

sauce

675 g/1 lb 8 oz fresh clams,
    or 280 g/10 oz canned clams,
    drained
2 tbsp olive oil
2 garlic cloves, finely chopped
400 g/14 oz mixed prepared
    seafood, such as prawns,
    squid and mussels, thawed
    if frozen
150 ml/5 fl oz white wine
150 ml/5 fl oz fish stock
2 tbsp chopped fresh tarragon
salt and pepper

method

1 First make the sauce. If you are using fresh clams, you need to scrub them clean and discard any that are already open.

2 Heat the oil in a large frying pan. Add the garlic and clams and cook for 2 minutes, shaking the pan to ensure that all of the clams are coated in the oil. Add the remaining seafood to the pan and cook for a further 2 minutes.

3 Pour the wine and stock over the mixed seafood and garlic and bring to the boil. Cover the pan, then lower the heat and simmer for 8–10 minutes, or until the shells open. Discard any clams or mussels that do not open.

4 To cook the pasta, place in a saucepan of boiling water, bring back to the boil and cook for 8–10 minutes, or until tender but still firm to the bite. Drain.

5 Stir the tarragon into the sauce and season to taste. Transfer the pasta to a serving plate and pour over the sauce.

spicy crab sauce

ingredients

serves 4

350 g/12 oz dried spaghettini
salt and pepper
lemon wedges, to garnish

sauce

1 dressed crab, about 450 g/1 lb
    (including the shell)
6 tbsp extra virgin olive oil
1 fresh red chilli, deseeded and
    finely chopped
2 garlic cloves, finely chopped
3 tbsp chopped fresh parsley
2 tbsp lemon juice
1 tsp finely grated lemon rind

method

1 Scoop the meat from the crab shell into a bowl. Mix the white and brown meat lightly together and set aside.

2 To cook the pasta, bring a large saucepan of lightly salted water to the boil. Add the pasta, bring back to the boil and cook for 8–10 minutes, or until tender but still firm to the bite. Drain well and return to the pan.

3 To make the sauce, heat 2 tablespoons of the olive oil in a frying pan. Add the chilli and garlic. Cook for 30 seconds, then add the crabmeat, parsley, lemon juice and lemon rind. Stir-fry over a low heat for a further 1 minute, or until the crab is heated through.

4 Add the crab sauce to the pasta with the remaining olive oil and season to taste with salt and pepper. Toss together thoroughly, transfer to a warmed serving dish and serve immediately, garnished with lemon wedges.

saffron mussel sauce

ingredients

serves 4

450 g/1 lb dried tagliatelle
1 tbsp olive oil
3 tbsp chopped fresh parsley,
    to garnish

sauce

1 kg/2 lb 4 oz mussels
150 ml/5 fl oz white wine
1 medium onion, finely chopped
2 tbsp butter
2 garlic cloves, crushed
2 tsp cornflour
300 ml/10 fl oz double cream
pinch of saffron threads or
    saffron powder
1 egg yolk
juice of ½ lemon
salt and pepper

method

1 Scrub and debeard the mussels under cold running water. Discard any that do not close when sharply tapped. Put the mussels in a saucepan with the wine and onion. Cover and cook over a high heat, shaking the pan, for 5–8 minutes, or until the shells open.

2 Drain and reserve the cooking liquid. Discard any mussels that are still closed. Reserve a few mussels in their shells for the garnish and remove the remainder from their shells. Strain the cooking liquid into a saucepan. Bring to the boil and reduce by about half. Remove from the heat.

3 Melt the butter in a saucepan. Add the garlic and fry, stirring frequently, for 2 minutes or until golden brown. Stir in the cornflour and cook, stirring, for 1 minute. Stir in the cooking liquid and the cream. Crush the saffron threads and add to the pan. Season with salt and pepper to taste and simmer over a low heat for 2–3 minutes, or until thickened. Stir in the egg yolk, lemon juice and mussels. Do not let the mixture boil.

4 To cook the pasta, bring a saucepan of lightly salted water to the boil. Add the pasta and oil and cook until tender but still firm to the bite. Drain and transfer to a serving dish. Add the mussel sauce. Garnish with chopped parsley and the reserved mussels and serve.

sardine & fennel sauce

ingredients

serves 4

350 g/12 oz dried linguine
2 tbsp olive oil
sprigs of fresh parsley, to garnish

sauce

8 sardines, filleted
1 fennel bulb
2 tbsp olive oil
3 garlic cloves, sliced
1 tsp chilli flakes
1/2 tsp finely grated lemon rind
1 tbsp lemon juice
2 tbsp pine kernels, toasted
2 tbsp chopped fresh parsley
salt and pepper

method

1 To make the sauce, wash the sardines and pat dry on kitchen paper. Coarsely chop them into large pieces and set aside. Trim the fennel bulb and slice very thinly.

2 Heat the olive oil in a large, heavy-based frying pan and add the sliced garlic and the chilli flakes. Cook for 1 minute, then add the fennel slices. Cook over a medium–high heat, stirring occasionally, for 4–5 minutes, or until softened. Lower the heat, add the sardine pieces and cook for a further 3–4 minutes, or until just cooked.

3 To cook the pasta, bring a saucepan of lightly salted water to the boil. Add the pasta, bring back to the boil and cook for 8–10 minutes, or until tender but still firm to the bite. Drain well and return to the pan.

4 Add the lemon rind and juice, pine kernels and parsley to the sauce and toss together. Season to taste with salt and pepper. Add the sauce to the pasta with the olive oil and toss together gently. Transfer to a warmed serving dish, garnish with parsley and serve.

spinach & anchovy sauce

ingredients

serves 4

400 g/14 oz dried fettucine
1 tbsp olive oil

sauce
900 g/2 lb fresh, young
　　spinach leaves
4 tbsp olive oil
3 tbsp pine kernels
3 garlic cloves, crushed
8 canned anchovy fillets,
　　drained and chopped

method

1 To make the sauce, trim off any tough spinach stalks. Rinse the spinach leaves and then place them in a large saucepan with only the water that is clinging to them after washing. Cover and cook over a high heat, shaking the pan from time to time, until the spinach has wilted but retains its colour. Drain well, set aside and keep warm.

2 To cook the pasta, bring a large saucepan of lightly salted water to the boil. Add the fettucine, bring back to the boil and cook for 8–10 minutes, or until tender but still firm to the bite.

3 Meanwhile, continue making the sauce. Heat the olive oil in a saucepan. Add the pine kernels and cook until golden. Remove the pine kernels from the pan with a slotted spoon and set aside.

4 Add the garlic to the pan and cook until golden. Add the anchovies and stir in the spinach. Cook, stirring constantly, for 2–3 minutes, or until heated through. Return the pine kernels to the pan.

5 Drain the fettucine, toss in the olive oil and transfer to a warmed serving dish. Spoon the spinach and anchovy sauce over the fettucine, then toss lightly and serve immediately.

smoked salmon & watercress sauce

ingredients

serves 4

225 g/8 oz dried fettuccine
1 tsp olive oil
1 garlic clove, finely chopped
55 g/2 oz smoked salmon,
    cut into thin strips
55 g/2 oz watercress leaves,
    plus extra to garnish
pepper

method

1 Bring a large saucepan of lightly salted water to the boil over a medium heat. Add the pasta, return to the boil and cook for 8–10 minutes, or until tender but still firm to the bite.

2 Meanwhile, heat the olive oil in a large non-stick frying pan. Add the garlic and cook over a low heat, stirring constantly, for 30 seconds. Add the salmon and watercress, season to taste with pepper and cook for a further 30 seconds, or until the watercress has wilted.

3 Drain the cooked pasta and return to the saucepan. Mix the salmon and watercress with the pasta, tossing the mixture using 2 large forks. Garnish with extra watercress leaves and serve immediately.

smoked salmon cream sauce

ingredients

serves 4

450 g/1 lb dried white or
    buckwheat spaghetti
2 tbsp olive oil
90 g/3¼ oz feta cheese, well
    drained and crumbled, and
    sprigs of fresh coriander or
    parsley, to garnish

sauce

300 ml/10 fl oz double cream
150 ml/5 fl oz whisky or brandy
125 g/4½ oz smoked salmon
pinch of cayenne pepper
black pepper
2 tbsp chopped fresh coriander
    or parsley

method

1 To cook the pasta, bring a large saucepan of lightly
    salted water to the boil. Add the spaghetti and half of
    the olive oil, bring back to the boil and cook for 8–10
    minutes, until tender but still firm to the bite. Drain the
    spaghetti, return to the pan and sprinkle over the
    remaining olive oil. Cover, shake the pan, set aside and
    keep warm.

2 To make the sauce, pour the cream into a small
    saucepan and bring to simmering point, but do not
    let it boil. Pour the whisky into another small saucepan
    and bring to simmering point, but do not let it boil.
    Remove both pans from the heat and mix the cream
    with the whisky.

3 Cut the smoked salmon into thin strips and add to the
    cream sauce. Season to taste with cayenne and black
    pepper. Just before serving, stir in the chopped fresh
    coriander. Transfer the spaghetti to a warmed serving
    dish, pour over the sauce and toss thoroughly with
    2 large forks. Garnish with feta cheese and fresh
    coriander and serve immediately.

creamy cheese sauce

ingredients

serves 4

25 g/1 oz butter
200 ml/7 fl oz double cream
450 g/1 lb dried fettuccine
1 tbsp olive oil
85 g/3 oz Parmesan cheese,
    freshly grated, plus extra
    to serve
pinch of freshly grated nutmeg
salt and pepper
fresh parsley sprigs, to garnish

method

1 Put the butter and 150 ml/5 fl oz of the cream in a large saucepan and bring the mixture to the boil over a medium heat. Reduce the heat and simmer gently for about 1½ minutes, or until slightly thickened.

2 Meanwhile, bring a large pan of lightly salted water to the boil. Add the fettuccine and olive oil, bring back to the boil and cook for 8–10 minutes, or until tender but still firm to the bite. Drain the fettuccine, then pour over the cream sauce.

3 Toss the fettuccine in the sauce over a low heat until thoroughly coated.

4 Add the remaining cream, the Parmesan cheese and nutmeg to the fettuccine mixture and season to taste with salt and pepper. Toss thoroughly to coat while gently heating through.

5 Transfer the fettuccine mixture to a warmed serving plate and garnish with the fresh sprigs of parsley. Serve immediately, handing round extra grated Parmesan cheese separately.

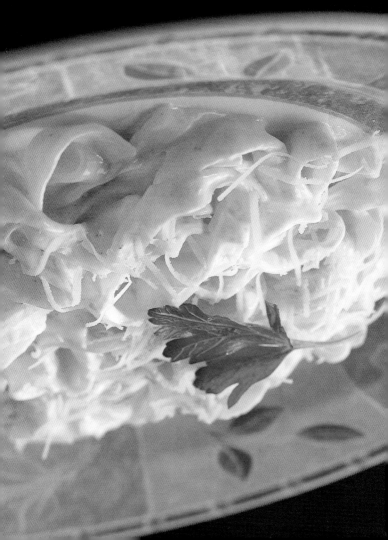

ricotta sauce

ingredients

serves 4

350 g/12 oz dried spaghetti
3 tbsp butter
2 tbsp chopped fresh flat-leaf
    parsley
115 g/4 oz freshly ground almonds
115 g/4 oz ricotta cheese
pinch of freshly grated nutmeg
pinch of ground cinnamon
150 ml/5 fl oz crème fraîche
2 tbsp olive oil
125 ml/4 fl oz hot chicken stock
1 tbsp pine kernels
salt and pepper
sprigs of fresh flat-leaf parsley,
    to garnish

method

1 Bring a saucepan of lightly salted water to the boil. Add the spaghetti, bring back to the boil and then cook for 8–10 minutes, or until tender but still firm to the bite.

2 Drain the pasta, return to the pan and toss with the butter and chopped parsley. Set aside and keep warm.

3 Combine the ground almonds, ricotta cheese, nutmeg, cinnamon and crème fraîche in a small saucepan and stir over a low heat to a thick paste. Gradually stir in the oil. When the oil has been fully incorporated, gradually stir in the hot stock until smooth. Season to taste with pepper.

4 Transfer the spaghetti to a warm serving dish, pour the sauce over it and toss together well. Sprinkle over the pine kernels, garnish with the sprigs of fresh flat-leaf parsley and serve immediately.

gorgonzola sauce

ingredients

serves 4

25 g/1 oz butter

225 g/8 oz Gorgonzola cheese,
    roughly crumbled

150 ml/5 fl oz double cream

2 tbsp dry white wine

1 tsp cornflour

4 fresh sage sprigs, finely
    chopped, plus extra to garnish

400 g/14 oz dried tagliarini

2 tbsp olive oil

salt and white pepper

method

1 Melt the butter in a heavy-based saucepan. Stir in
   175 g/6 oz of the cheese and melt, over a low heat,
   for about 2 minutes.

2 Add the cream, white wine and cornflour and beat
   with a whisk until fully incorporated.

3 Stir in the sage and season to taste with salt and white
   pepper. Bring to the boil over a low heat, whisking
   constantly, until the sauce thickens. Remove from the
   heat and set aside while you cook the pasta.

4 Bring a large saucepan of lightly salted water to the
   boil. Add the tagliarini and 1 tablespoon of the olive
   oil, bring back to the boil and cook for 8–10 minutes, o
   until tender but still firm to the bite. Drain thoroughly
   and toss in the remaining olive oil. Transfer the pasta to
   a serving dish and keep warm.

5 Reheat the gorgonzola sauce over a low heat,
   whisking constantly. Spoon the sauce over the
   tagliarini. Generously sprinkle over the remaining
   cheese, garnish with sage leaves and serve immediately.

creamy mushroom sauce

ingredients

serves 4

450 g/1 lb dried spaghetti
1 tbsp olive oil
1 tbsp coarsely chopped fresh
   parsley
12 triangles of fried white
   bread, to serve

sauce

55 g/2 oz butter
1 tbsp olive oil
6 shallots, sliced
450 g/1 lb button
   mushrooms, sliced
1 tsp plain flour
150 ml/5 fl oz double cream
2 tbsp port
115 g/4 oz sun-dried
   tomatoes, chopped
pinch of freshly grated nutmeg
salt and pepper

method

1 To make the sauce, heat the butter and olive oil in a
   large saucepan. Add the sliced shallots and cook over
   a medium heat for 3 minutes. Add the mushrooms and
   cook over a low heat for 2 minutes. Season to taste
   with salt and pepper, then sprinkle over the flour and
   cook, stirring constantly, for 1 minute.

2 Gradually stir in the cream and port, then add the
   sun-dried tomatoes and a pinch of grated nutmeg.
   Cook over a low heat for 8 minutes.

3 Meanwhile, to cook the pasta, bring a large saucepan
   of lightly salted water to the boil. Add the spaghetti
   and olive oil, bring back to the boil and cook for
   8–10 minutes, or until tender but still firm to the bite.

4 Drain the spaghetti and return to the pan. Pour over
   the mushroom sauce and cook for 3 minutes. Transfer
   the spaghetti and mushroom sauce to a large serving
   plate and sprinkle over the chopped parsley. Serve
   with crispy triangles of fried bread.

creamy butternut squash sauce

ingredients

serves 4

2 tbsp olive oil
1 garlic clove, crushed
55 g/2 oz fresh white breadcrumbs
500 g/1 lb 2 oz butternut squash,
    peeled and deseeded
4 tbsp water
500 g/1 lb 2 oz fresh penne,
    or other pasta shapes
15 g/½ oz butter
1 onion, sliced
125 g/4½ oz ham, cut into strips
200 ml/7 fl oz single cream
55 g/2 oz freshly grated
    Cheddar cheese
2 tbsp chopped fresh parsley
salt and pepper

method

1 Heat the olive oil in a saucepan and fry the garlic and breadcrumbs gently over a medium–low heat, until crisp. Set aside.

2 Dice the squash and cook in a large saucepan of boiling water for 8–10 minutes, or until soft. Drain and set aside.

3 Meanwhile, bring a large saucepan of lightly salted water to the boil. Add the pasta, bring back to the boil and cook for 8–10 minutes, or until tender but still firm to the bite.

4 Melt the butter in a large frying pan, add the onion and fry over a low heat until soft. Using a fork, coarsely mash the squash. Add to the onion with the ham, cream, cheese, parsley and water. Drain the pasta thoroughly and add to the pan. Season to taste with salt and pepper and mix well. Allow to cook until heated through.

5 Transfer the pasta to a large warmed serving dish, sprinkle with the garlic crumbs and serve.

blue cheese & broccoli sauce

ingredients

serves 4

300 g/10½ oz dried tagliatelle
   tricolore (plain, spinach- and
   tomato-flavoured noodles)
225 g/8 oz broccoli, broken into
   small florets
350 g/12 oz mascarpone cheese
125 g/4½ oz chopped blue cheese
1 tbsp chopped fresh oregano
25 g/1 oz butter
salt and pepper
sprigs of fresh oregano, to garnish
freshly grated Parmesan cheese,
   to serve

method

1 To cook the pasta, bring a large saucepan of lightly
   salted water to the boil. Add the pasta, bring back to
   the boil and cook for 8–10 minutes, or until tender but
   still firm to the bite.

2 Meanwhile, cook the broccoli florets in a small amount
   of lightly salted, boiling water. Avoid overcooking the
   broccoli, so that it retains its colour and texture.

3 Heat the mascarpone and blue cheeses together
   gently in a large saucepan until they are melted. Stir in
   the oregano and season with salt and pepper to taste.

4 Drain the pasta thoroughly. Return it to the saucepan
   and add the butter, tossing the tagliatelle to coat it.
   Drain the broccoli well and add to the pasta with the
   sauce, tossing gently to mix.

5 Divide the pasta between four warmed serving plates.
   Garnish with sprigs of fresh oregano and serve with
   freshly grated Parmesan cheese.

buttered pea & cheese sauce

ingredients

serves 4

450 g/1 lb mixed dried green and
white spaghetti or tagliatelle
2 tbsp Parmesan cheese shavings,
to garnish

sauce

55 g/2 oz butter
450 g/1 lb fresh peas, shelled
200 ml/7 fl oz double cream
55 g/2 oz Parmesan cheese,
freshly grated
pinch of freshly grated nutmeg
salt and pepper

method

1 To make the sauce, melt the butter in a large saucepan. Add the peas and cook over a low heat for 2–3 minutes. Pour 150 ml/5 fl oz of the cream into the pan, bring to the boil and then simmer for 1–1½ minutes, or until slightly thickened. Remove the pan from the heat.

2 Meanwhile, to cook the pasta, bring a large saucepan of lightly salted water to the boil. Add the pasta, bring back to the boil and cook for 8–10 minutes, or until tender but still firm to the bite. Remove the pan from the heat, drain the pasta thoroughly and return to the pan.

3 Add the sauce to the pasta. Return the pan to the heat and add the remaining cream and the Parmesan cheese, using 2 forks to toss the pasta gently so that it is coated with the sauce. Season to taste with nutmeg and salt and pepper.

4 Transfer the pasta to a large warmed serving dish. Garnish with Parmesan cheese and serve immediately.

green vegetable sauce

ingredients

serves 4

225 g/8 oz dried gemelli or other
    dried pasta shapes
1 head broccoli, cut into florets
2 courgettes, sliced
225 g/8 oz asparagus spears
115 g/4 oz mangetout
115 g/4 oz frozen peas
25 g/1 oz butter
3 tbsp vegetable stock
4 tbsp double cream
freshly grated nutmeg
2 tbsp chopped fresh parsley
salt and pepper
2 tbsp Parmesan cheese shavings,
    to garnish

method

1 Bring a large saucepan of lightly salted water to the
boil over a medium heat. Add the pasta, bring back to
the boil and cook for 8–10 minutes, or until tender but
still firm to the bite. Drain thoroughly, return to the pan,
cover and keep warm.

2 Steam the broccoli, courgettes, asparagus spears and
mangetout over a saucepan of boiling salted water
until they are just starting to soften. Remove from the
heat and refresh in cold water. Drain and reserve.

3 Bring a small saucepan of lightly salted water to the
boil over a medium heat. Add the frozen peas and
cook for 3 minutes. Drain the peas, refresh in cold water,
then drain again. Reserve with the other vegetables.

4 Heat the butter and vegetable stock in a saucepan
over a medium heat. Add all of the vegetables,
reserving a few of the asparagus spears, and toss
carefully with a wooden spoon until they have heated
through, taking care not to break them up. Stir in the
cream and heat through without bringing to the boil.
Season to taste with salt and pepper and nutmeg.

5 Transfer the pasta to a warmed serving dish and stir in
the chopped parsley. Spoon over the vegetable sauce
and sprinkle over the Parmesan cheese. Arrange the
reserved asparagus spears on the top and serve.

hot courgette sauce

ingredients

serves 4

225 g/8 oz dried tagliatelle
crusty bread, to serve

sauce

675 g/1 lb 8 oz courgettes
6 tbsp olive oil
3 garlic cloves, crushed
3 tbsp chopped fresh basil
2 fresh red chillies, deseeded
    and sliced
juice of 1 large lemon
5 tbsp single cream
4 tbsp grated Parmesan cheese
salt and pepper

method

1 To make the sauce, use a swivel-bladed vegetable peeler to slice the courgettes into thin ribbons.

2 Heat the oil in a frying pan and cook the garlic for 30 seconds. Add the courgettes and cook over a low heat, stirring, for 5–7 minutes. Stir in the basil, chillies, lemon juice, cream and Parmesan cheese and season to taste with salt and pepper. Keep warm over a very low heat.

3 To cook the pasta, bring a large saucepan of lightly salted water to the boil. Add the pasta, bring back to the boil and cook for 8–10 minutes, or until tender but still firm to the bite. Drain thoroughly and put the pasta in a warmed serving bowl.

4 Pile the courgette sauce on top of the pasta and serve immediately with crusty bread.

fragrant aubergine sauce

ingredients

serves 4

150 ml/5 fl oz vegetable stock
150 ml/5 fl oz white wine vinegar
2 tsp balsamic vinegar
3 tbsp olive oil
sprig of fresh oregano
450 g/1 lb aubergines, peeled
    and thinly sliced
400 g/14 oz dried linguine

marinade

2 tbsp extra virgin olive oil
2 garlic cloves, crushed
2 tbsp chopped fresh oregano
2 tbsp finely chopped roasted
    almonds
2 tbsp diced red pepper
2 tbsp lime juice
grated rind and juice of 1 orange
salt and pepper

method

1 Put the vegetable stock, wine vinegar and balsamic vinegar into a saucepan and bring to the boil over a low heat. Add 2 teaspoons of the olive oil and the sprig of fresh oregano and simmer gently for about 1 minute. Add the sliced aubergine slices to the pan, remove from the heat and set aside for 10 minutes.

2 Meanwhile, to make the marinade, combine all the ingredients in a large bowl and season to taste with salt and pepper.

3 Using a slotted spoon, carefully remove the aubergine slices from the pan and drain well. Add the aubergine to the marinade, mixing well to coat. Cover with clingfilm and set aside in the refrigerator for about 12 hours.

4 To cook the pasta, bring a large saucepan of lightly salted water to the boil. Add half of the remaining oil and the linguine. Bring back to the boil and cook for 8–10 minutes, or until tender but still firm to the bite.

5 Drain the pasta thoroughly and toss with the remaining oil while it is still warm. Arrange the pasta on a serving plate with the aubergine slices and the marinade on top. Serve immediately.

garlic walnut sauce

ingredients

serves 4

450 g/1 lb dried green and
    white tagliatelle
sprigs of fresh basil, to garnish
salt and pepper
Italian bread, such as focaccia
    or ciabatta, to serve

sauce

2 tbsp walnut oil
1 bunch of spring onions, sliced
2 garlic cloves, thinly sliced
225 g/8 oz mushrooms, sliced
225 g/8 oz frozen spinach,
    thawed and drained
115 g/4 oz full-fat cream cheese
    with garlic and herbs
4 tbsp single cream
55 g/2 oz unsalted pistachio nuts,
    chopped
2 tbsp shredded fresh basil
salt and pepper

method

1 To make the sauce, heat the walnut oil in a large
    frying pan. Add the spring onions and garlic and fry
    for 1 minute, or until just softened.

2 Add the sliced mushrooms, stir well, cover and cook
    over a low heat for 5 minutes, or until just softened but
    not browned.

3 Meanwhile, to cook the pasta, bring a large saucepan
    of lightly salted water to the boil. Add the tagliatelle,
    bring back to the boil and cook for 8–10 minutes, or
    until tender but still firm to the bite. Drain thoroughly
    and return to the pan.

4 Add the spinach to the frying pan and cook for 1–2
    minutes. Add the cheese and heat until slightly melted.
    Stir in the cream and cook gently, without letting the
    mixture come to the boil, until warmed through.

5 Pour the sauce over the pasta, season to taste with salt
    and pepper and mix well. Heat through gently, stirring
    constantly, for 2–3 minutes.

6 Transfer the pasta to a warmed serving dish and sprinkle
    with the pistachio nuts and shredded basil. Garnish with
    fresh basil sprigs and serve immediately with Italian
    bread of your choice.

olive oil & herb sauce

ingredients

serves 4

125 ml/4 fl oz olive oil
3 garlic cloves, crushed
450 g/1 lb fresh spaghetti
3 tbsp roughly chopped
    fresh parsley
salt and pepper

method

1 Reserve 1 tablespoon of the olive oil and heat the remainder in a medium saucepan. Add the garlic and a pinch of salt and cook over a low heat, stirring constantly, until golden brown, then remove the pan from the heat. Do not allow the garlic to burn as this will taint its flavour.

2 Meanwhile, bring a large saucepan of lightly salted water to the boil. Add the spaghetti and remaining olive oil, bring back to the boil and cook for 2–3 minutes, or until tender but still firm to the bite. Drain the spaghetti thoroughly and return to the pan.

3 Add the oil and garlic mixture to the spaghetti and toss to coat thoroughly. Season to taste with pepper, add the chopped fresh parsley and toss well to coat again.

4 Transfer the spaghetti to a warmed serving dish and serve immediately.

dressings

garlic vinaigrette

ingredients

*makes about 150 ml/
5 fl oz*

125 ml/4 fl oz garlic-flavoured
olive oil
3 tbsp white wine vinegar
or lemon juice
1–2 garlic cloves, crushed
1 tsp Dijon mustard
½ tsp caster sugar
salt and pepper, to taste

method

1 Put all the ingredients in a screw-top jar, secure the
lid and shake vigorously until an emulsion forms.
Taste and adjust the seasoning if necessary.

2 Use at once or store in an airtight container in the
refrigerator for up to a month. Strain to remove the
garlic cloves after 1 week. Always whisk or shake the
dressing before using.

herb vinaigrette

ingredients

makes about 150 ml/
5 fl oz

125 ml/4 fl oz olive or other
    vegetable oil
3 tbsp white wine vinegar
    or lemon juice
1½ tbsp chopped fresh herbs,
    such as chives, parsley or mint
1 tsp Dijon mustard
½ tsp caster sugar
salt and pepper, to taste

method

1 Put all the ingredients in a screw-top jar, secure the
   lid and shake vigorously until a thick emulsion forms.
   Taste and adjust the seasoning if necessary.

2 Use at once or store in an airtight container in the
   refrigerator for up to 3 days. Always whisk or shake
   the dressing before using, and strain through a fine
   non-metallic sieve if the herbs begin to darken.

dill & peppercorn vinegar

ingredients

makes about 225 ml/
8 fl oz

225 ml/8 fl oz cider vinegar
6 sprigs fresh dill
1 tsp whole black peppercorns

method

1 Put the vinegar in a saucepan over a medium heat and bring to the boil. Reduce the heat and simmer for 2 minutes. Add the dill and peppercorns, turn off the heat and leave to stand for several minutes until cool.

2 Pour into a clean jar, seal and refrigerate or keep in a dark place. The vinegar can be used to make a classic oil and vinegar dressing as required.

garlic, chilli & oregano oil

ingredients

*makes about 225 ml/
8 fl oz*

5 garlic cloves, halved lengthways

2 tbsp deseeded and chopped
red hot chilli

1 tsp dried oregano

225 ml/8 fl oz rapeseed oil

method

1 Preheat the oven to 150°C/300°F/Gas Mark 2. Combine the garlic, chilli and oregano with the oil in an ovenproof glass measuring jug. Place on a glass pie plate in the centre of the oven and heat for 1½–2 hours. The temperature of the oil should reach 120°C/250°F.

2 Remove from the oven, allow to cool, then strain through muslin into a clean jar. Store, covered, in the refrigerator. You can also leave the garlic and chilli pieces in the oil and strain before using. The oil can be used to make a classic oil and vinegar dressing as required.

basil, chive & lemon dressing

ingredients

makes 600 ml/
1 pint

450–675 g/1–1½ lb small
    potatoes, skins on

5 cooked artichoke hearts

55 g/2 oz chopped dill pickles

1 tbsp fresh dill, chopped

20 chives, snipped

4 tbsp basil, chive and lemon
    vinegar

1 tsp Dijon mustard

2 tbsp olive oil

1 tbsp fresh lemon juice

salt and pepper

method

1 Bring a large saucepan of lightly salted water to
  the boil, add the potatoes and cook until soft. Cut
  into bite-sized pieces. Cut the artichoke hearts into
  bite-sized pieces and combine in a mixing bowl
  with the potatoes. Add the pickles, dill and chives.

2 Whisk the vinegar, mustard, oil and lemon juice
  together. Season to taste with salt and pepper. Pour
  over the potato and artichoke mixture and mix.

3 Serve immediately or store, covered, in the refrigerator
  and bring to room temperature before serving.

roasted pepper & garlic dressing

ingredients

makes about 150ml/
5 fl oz

85 g/3 oz deseeded red
    pepper, halved
½ tsp rapeseed or vegetable oil
2 tbsp sliced garlic
1 tbsp coriander seeds
1 tsp cumin seeds
2 tsp chopped fresh rosemary
100 ml/3½ fl oz water
1 tsp sugar
¼ tsp smoked paprika
1 tbsp white wine vinegar
1 tbsp cornflour, blended with a
    little cold water

method

1 Preheat the oven to 200°C/400°F/Gas Mark 6. Put the pepper on a non-stick baking sheet and roast in the oven until the skin blisters. Remove from the oven, leave to cool, then peel off the skin.

2 Heat the oil in a small saucepan over a medium heat, add the garlic and cook, stirring constantly, until golden brown. Add the coriander seeds and cumin seeds and cook for 1 minute, stirring. Add the rosemary water, sugar, paprika and vinegar and bring to the boil. Gradually add the cornflour, stirring constantly, and cook until thickened.

3 Add the roasted pepper, put in a food processor and process until smooth. Pass through a fine sieve, cover with clingfilm to prevent a skin forming and leave to cool. Store, covered, in the refrigerator.

green dressing

ingredients

*makes about 350 ml/
12 fl oz*

300 ml/10 fl oz low-fat
    natural yogurt
2 tsp Dijon mustard
2–3 tbsp white wine vinegar
4 tsp sunflower oil
2 tbsp coarsely chopped
    fresh parsley
2 tbsp snipped fresh chives
2 tbsp coarsely chopped
    fresh tarragon
1 spring onion, coarsely chopped
1 tbsp coarsely chopped watercress
salt and pepper

method

1 Put the yogurt, mustard, vinegar and oil into a food
processor and season to taste with salt and pepper.
Process on medium speed until thoroughly combined.

2 Add the parsley, chives, tarragon, spring onion and
watercress and process for a few seconds to chop
finely and blend. Serve immediately.

slim-line dressing

ingredients

makes about 300ml/
10 fl oz

300 ml/10 fl oz low-fat
   natural yogurt
1 tsp English mustard
2–3 tbsp lemon juice
4 tsp sunflower oil
salt and pepper

method

1 Put all the ingredients into a food processor, season
   to taste with salt and pepper and process on medium
   speed until thoroughly combined. Store, covered, in
   the refrigerator.

tomato dressing

ingredients

makes about 125 ml/
4 fl oz

2 tbsp balsamic vinegar, or red
    or white wine vinegar
4–6 tbsp extra virgin olive oil
1 tsp Dijon mustard
pinch of caster sugar
1 tbsp torn fresh basil leaves
1 tbsp chopped sun-dried
    tomatoes
salt and pepper

method

1 Place all the ingredients in a screw-top jar, secure
    the top and shake well. Alternatively, beat all the
    ingredients together in a small bowl. Use as much
    oil as you like. If you have just salad leaves to dress,
    4 tablespoons of oil will be sufficient, but if you have
    heavier ingredients such as potatoes, you will need
    about 6 tablespoons of oil.

2 Use the dressing at once. If you want to store it, do not
    add the basil – it will then keep for about 3–4 days in
    the refrigerator.

sweet & sour dressing

ingredients

makes about 125 ml/
4 fl oz

2 tbsp lemon juice, or red or
white wine vinegar

4–6 tbsp extra virgin olive oil

1 tsp Dijon mustard

pinch of caster sugar

1 tbsp honey

1 tsp finely grated fresh ginger

1 tbsp toasted sesame seeds

1 tbsp chopped fresh parsley

salt and pepper

method

1 Place all the ingredients in a screw-top jar, secure
the top and shake well. Alternatively, beat all the
ingredients together in a small bowl. Use as much
oil as you like. A dressing for salad leaves will require
4 tablespoons of oil, but heavier ingredients, such
as potatoes, will require about 6 tablespoons of oil.
Serve immediately.

honey & yogurt dressing

ingredients

makes about 125 ml/
4 fl oz

1 tbsp clear honey, plus
    extra to drizzle
90 ml/3 fl oz low-fat
    natural yogurt
salt and pepper

method

1 Put the honey and yogurt in a glass bowl and beat with
    a fork until thoroughly combined. Season to taste with
    salt and pepper and drizzle over a little extra honey.
    Serve immediately.

variation

To make a honey mustard yogurt dressing, add
1–2 tablespoons of sweet honey mustard, available from
a delicatessen, and mix in well.

pink grapefruit, raspberry, wasabi & sesame oil dressing

ingredients

*makes about 125 ml/
4 fl oz*

1 pink grapefruit, halved

75 ml/2½ fl oz water

1 tbsp white wine vinegar

1 tsp sugar

1 tbsp cornflour, blended with
a little cold water

25 g/1 oz raspberries

¼ tsp wasabi paste

1 tsp sesame oil

method

1 Working over a bowl, cut the skin and white pith off the grapefruit and cut the grapefruit segments between the membranes. Reserve 85 g/3 oz of the segments and squeeze 85 ml/3 fl oz of the juice from the remainder.

2 Put the grapefruit juice, water, vinegar and sugar into a small saucepan over a medium heat and bring to the boil. Gradually add the cornflour mixture, stirring. Cook until thick, then remove from the heat. Add the grapefruit, raspberries, wasabi paste and oil.

3 Put the mixture into a food processor and process until smooth. Pass through a fine sieve. Cover with clingfilm and chill in the refrigerator. Keep the dressing in the refrigerator until ready to use.

salsas

tomato salsa

ingredients

makes about 300 g/
10¹⁄₂ oz

4 ripe tomatoes, about 225 g/
    8 oz total weight
1 small red onion
1 fresh red jalapeño chilli,
    deseeded
1–2 garlic cloves, crushed
5-cm/2-inch piece cucumber
1 tsp (or to taste) clear honey
1 tbsp chopped fresh coriander
pepper
tortilla chips, to serve

method

1 Deseed the tomatoes, finely chop and put in a small non-metallic bowl. Finely chop the onion and chilli and add to the tomatoes with the garlic.

2 Peel the cucumber with a swivel-bladed vegetable peeler. Cut in half lengthways and scoop out and discard the seeds. Finely chop the flesh and add to the bowl with the honey and pepper to taste.

3 Add the coriander and stir well. Lightly cover and leave to stand in a cool place, but not the refrigerator, for 30 minutes to let the flavours develop. Serve with tortilla chips.

warm tomatillo salsa

ingredients

makes about 400 g/
14 oz

1 small red pepper
1 small green pepper
1–2 (or to taste) fresh red
    jalapeño chillies
1 tbsp olive oil
2–3 garlic cloves, crushed
2 shallots, finely chopped
225 g/8 oz tomatillos
1 tbsp chopped fresh coriander
2 tsp maple syrup
1 tbsp (or to taste) tequila
pepper
tortillas, to serve

method

1 Preheat the grill to high and line the grill rack with foil. Cut the red and green peppers into quarters and remove and discard the seeds and membranes. Put on the foil-lined grill rack with the chilli. Cook under the preheated grill for 10 minutes, or until the skins are charred and blistered, turning the chilli occasionally.

2 Remove from the heat, transfer the peppers and chillies to a polythene bag and leave to cool for 10 minutes. Peel away the skins from the peppers. Peel away the skin from the chilli, cut in half and remove and discard the seeds and membrane. Finely chop the peppers and chilli.

3 Heat the oil in a heavy-based saucepan, add the garlic and shallots and gently sauté, stirring frequently, for 5 minutes. Add the chopped peppers and chilli.

4 Cut the tomatillos into quarters and finely chop the flesh. Add to the saucepan with the remaining ingredients. Heat gently, stirring occasionally, for 5–8 minutes until thoroughly heated through. Serve warm with tortillas.

three bean salsa

ingredients

makes about 300 g/
10½ oz

55 g/2 oz fresh or frozen
    broad beans
55 g/2 oz French beans,
    roughly chopped
2 tbsp olive oil
2 shallots, finely chopped
1–3 garlic cloves, crushed
1 fresh red serrano chilli,
    deseeded and finely chopped
3 tbsp canned red kidney
    beans, rinsed, drained
    and roughly chopped
2 tomatoes, about 115 g/4 oz,
    roughly chopped
2 tbsp canned pickled chillies,
    drained and finely chopped
1 tsp (or to taste) clear honey
1 tbsp chopped fresh coriander
salt
tacos, to serve

method

1 Cook the broad beans with the French beans in a
    saucepan of boiling water for 4–5 minutes until tender.
    Drain well.

2 Heat the oil in a small heavy-based saucepan, add the
    shallots, garlic and fresh chilli and gently sauté, stirring
    frequently, for 5 minutes.

3 Add the cooked beans with the kidney beans,
    tomatoes, pickled chillies and honey. Heat over a
    medium heat, stirring occasionally, for 5–8 minutes
    until thoroughly heated through. Stir in the coriander
    and serve warm in tacos.

avocado salsa

ingredients

makes about 425 g/
15 oz

2 ripe tomatoes,
    about 115 g/4 oz
    total weight
2 ripe avocados
3 tbsp freshly squeezed
    lime juice
6 spring onions
2–3 garlic cloves, crushed
1 fresh red serrano chilli,
    deseeded and finely chopped
1 celery stick, finely chopped
3 tbsp canned red kidney beans,
    rinsed, drained and roughly
    chopped
1 tsp clear honey
1 tbsp chopped fresh coriander
pepper

method

1 Make a cross in the stalk end of each tomato, put in
   a heatproof bowl and pour over boiling water to
   cover. Leave to stand for 2 minutes, then remove with
   a slotted spoon and leave to cool. When cool enough
   to handle, peel away the skins. Cut into quarters,
   deseed and finely chop.

2 Cut the avocados in half and remove and discard the
   stones. Peel, then finely chop the flesh and put in a
   separate bowl. Pour over the lime juice and gently stir
   until the avocados are thoroughly coated in the lime
   juice. Stir in the chopped tomatoes.

3 Finely chop the spring onions and add to the bowl
   with the garlic, chilli and celery. Add the beans to the
   bowl with the honey, pepper to taste and coriander.
   Stir well and transfer to a non-metallic serving bowl.
   Lightly cover and leave to stand in a cool place, but
   not the refrigerator, for 30 minutes to let all the
   flavours develop before serving.

roasted corn salsa

ingredients

makes about 500 g/
1 lb 2 oz

2 corn cobs
1 tbsp unsalted butter, melted
4 garlic cloves, crushed
2 fresh red serrano chillies,
    deseeded and finely chopped
115 g/4 oz broccoli, blanched and
    finely chopped into tiny florets
1 red onion, finely chopped
2 ripe tomatoes, about 115 g/4 oz,
    peeled and finely chopped
1 tsp (or to taste) white
    wine vinegar
1–2 tsp maple syrup
1 tbsp chopped fresh mint
filled tortillas topped with melted
    cheese, to serve

method

1 Preheat the oven to 180°C/350°F/Gas Mark 4. Remove and discard the outer leaves and silky threads from the corn cobs and lightly rinse. Put each cob on a 15-cm/6-inch square of foil.

2 Lightly brush each cob with the melted butter, then sprinkle over the garlic and chillies. Lift the sides of each foil square up and fold over at the top to encase the cobs, transfer to a roasting tin and roast in the preheated oven for 20–30 minutes until tender. Remove from the oven and leave to cool.

3 When the cobs are cool enough to handle, strip off the kernels with a knife and put in a small bowl. Add all the remaining ingredients and stir well. Lightly cover and leave to stand in a cool place, but not the refrigerator, for 30 minutes to let the flavours develop.

4 Gently reheat the mixture, stirring occasionally, for 5–8 minutes. Serve warm with filled tortillas, topped with melted cheese.

mexican salsa

ingredients

makes about 325 g/
11½ oz

1–2 (or to taste) dried ancho
    chillies
1–2 (or to taste) fresh red serrano
    chillies
1–2 (or to taste) fresh green
    serrano chillies
1 courgette, about 115 g/4 oz
4 ripe tomatoes, about
    225 g/8 oz total weight
2 tsp maple syrup
1 tbsp freshly squeezed lime juice
1 tbsp chopped fresh coriander
warmed tortillas and lime wedges,
    to serve

method

1 Put the dried chilli in a heatproof bowl, cover with
    almost boiling water and leave to soak for 20 minutes.
    Drain well and then finely chop.

2 Cut the fresh chillies in half and remove and discard
    the seeds and membranes. Finely chop the flesh and
    put in a bowl with the chopped dried chillies.

3 Coarsely grate the courgette and add to the chillies.
    Cut the tomatoes into quarters, deseed and finely
    chop the flesh. Add to the chillies with the remaining
    ingredients. Stir well and spoon into a non-metallic
    serving dish. Lightly cover and leave to stand in a
    cool place, but not the refrigerator, for 30 minutes
    to let the flavours develop. Stir again and serve in
    warmed tortillas with lime wedges.

tex-mex salsa

ingredients

*makes about 400 g/
14 oz*

1 large avocado
2 tbsp freshly squeezed
    lime juice
1 white onion, coarsely grated
1–3 (or to taste) fresh green
    jalapeño chillies
1–2 tsp maple syrup
55 g/2 oz canned pinto beans,
    rinsed and drained
225 g/8 oz ripe tomatoes,
    peeled if preferred
1 tbsp chopped fresh coriander
tortilla chips and melted cheese,
    to serve

method

1 Cut the avocado in half and remove and discard the
   stone. Peel, then finely chop the flesh. Put in a bowl.
   Pour over the lime juice and gently stir until the
   avocado is thoroughly coated. Stir in the onion.

2 Cut the chilli in half and remove and discard the seeds
   and membrane. Finely chop the flesh. Add to the
   avocado with the maple syrup.

3 Roughly chop the pinto beans and add to the bowl.
   Cut the tomatoes into quarters, deseed and finely
   chop the flesh. Add to the bowl with the coriander.

4 Stir the salsa well and spoon into a non-metallic
   serving dish. Lightly cover and leave to stand in a
   cool place, but not the refrigerator, for 30 minutes to
   let the flavours develop. Serve with tortilla chips and
   melted cheese.

apple & habanero chilli salsa

ingredients

makes about 400 g/14 oz

1 small orange pepper
1 small green pepper
1 green eating apple
2 tbsp freshly squeezed
  lemon juice
1–2 (or to taste) fresh
  habanero chillies
6 spring onions, finely chopped
1 tbsp maple syrup
2–3 tsp (or to taste) hot pepper
  sauce
1 tbsp chopped fresh mint
grilled pork chops, to serve

method

1 Preheat the grill and line the grill rack with foil. Cut the orange and green peppers into quarters and remove and discard the seeds and membranes. Put on the foil-lined grill rack and cook under the preheated grill for 10 minutes, or until the pepper skins are charred and blistered.

2 Remove from the heat, transfer to a polythene bag and leave to cool for 10 minutes. Peel away the skins and finely chop the flesh.

3 Cut the apple into quarters and cut away and discard the core. Coarsely grate the flesh and put in a bowl. Pour over the lemon juice and stir well until the apple is coated in the lemon juice. Add the peppers.

4 Cut the chilli in half, remove and discard the seeds and membrane and finely chop. Add to the apple and peppers with all the remaining ingredients. Stir well and spoon into a non-metallic serving dish. Lightly cover and leave to stand in a cool place, but not the refrigerator, for at least 30 minutes to let the flavours develop. Stir again and serve with grilled pork chops.

chilli & garlic salsa

ingredients

makes about 350 g/12 oz

4 garlic cloves
1–3 fresh red serrano chillies
25–55 g/1–2 oz pickled chillies,
    drained and finely chopped
1 large courgette, about
    175 g/6 oz, grated
1 large carrot, about 175 g/6 oz,
    peeled and grated
2 tsp soy sauce
1 tsp clear honey
1 tbsp chopped fresh coriander
grilled pork chops, to serve

method

1 Finely crush the garlic and put in a small bowl. Cut the fresh chillies in half, remove and discard the seeds and membranes, and finely chop. Alternatively, if a hotter salsa is preferred, leave the seeds and membranes in place and finely chop. Add to the garlic with the pickled chillies.

2 Stir the courgette and carrot into the bowl with the soy sauce and honey. Add the coriander and stir well.

3 Transfer the salsa to a small saucepan and gently heat, stirring occasionally, for 3–5 minutes before serving with grilled pork chops.

caribbean salsa

ingredients

makes about 600 g/
1 lb 5 oz

1 small ripe mango, peeled
1 small ripe papaya, peeled
1–2 (or to taste) fresh
    habanero chillies
4 spring onions, finely chopped
1–2 tsp maple syrup
½ small fresh coconut
1 tbsp chopped fresh coriander
pepper
grilled tuna steaks, to serve

method

1 Remove and discard the stone from the mango.
Finely chop the flesh and put in a bowl. Scoop out and
discard the seeds from the papaya. Finely chop the
flesh and add to the mango.

2 Cut the chilli in half, remove and discard the seeds and
membrane and finely chop. Add to the fruit with the
spring onions and maple syrup.

3 Discard any outer shell from the coconut, leaving the
white coconut flesh. Grate the coconut flesh. Add to
the fruit with the coriander and pepper to taste. Spoon
into a serving dish. Lightly cover and leave to stand
in a cool place, but not the refrigerator, for at least
30 minutes to let the flavours develop. Serve with
grilled tuna steaks.

creole pineapple salsa

ingredients

makes about 300 g/
10½ oz

7.5-cm/3-inch piece cucumber
1 tsp salt
½ small ripe fresh pineapple,
    about 115 g/4 oz peeled
    and cored weight
6 spring onions, chopped
1 fresh red Anaheim chilli,
    deseeded and finely chopped
1–2 tsp hot pepper sauce
1–2 tsp maple syrup
1 tbsp chopped fresh mint
25 g/1 oz unsalted cashew nuts,
    roughly chopped
stir-fried prawns, for serving

method

1 Peel the cucumber with a swivel-bladed vegetable
peeler and cut lengthways into quarters. Scoop out
and discard the seeds. Finely chop the flesh, put in a
non-metallic sieve and sprinkle with the salt. Leave to
drain for 15–20 minutes, then rinse thoroughly and
drain well. Put in a bowl.

2 Slice off the outer skin from the pineapple and cut
away and discard any central core. Either finely chop
the flesh with a large cook's knife or put in a food
processor and process for 1 minute, or until finely
chopped. Add to the cucumber with the spring onions
and chilli.

3 Add the hot pepper sauce with the maple syrup
and mint. Spoon into a serving dish. Lightly cover and
leave to stand in a cool place, but not the refrigerator,
for at least 30 minutes to let the flavours develop.
Sprinkle with the cashew nuts just before serving with
stir-fried prawns.

tropical salsa

ingredients

makes about 350 g/12 oz

1 small wedge watermelon,
about 115 g/4 oz
2 blood oranges, if available,
or 1 red grapefruit
1–2 fresh green jalapeño chillies
2 tsp clear honey
55 g/2 oz stem ginger, drained,
plus 2–3 tsp syrup from the jar
1 tbsp chopped fresh mint
chicken or fish kebabs, to serve

method

1 Peel the watermelon, deseed and finely chop. Put in
a bowl. Working over the bowl to catch the juices, peel
the oranges, removing and discarding all the bitter
white pith. Separate into segments, chop the flesh and
add to the watermelon.

2 Cut the chillies in half, remove and discard the seeds
and membrane, and finely chop. Add to the fruit with
the honey. Stir well.

3 Finely chop the stem ginger and add to the bowl with
the ginger syrup. Add the mint and stir well. Transfer
the salsa to a serving bowl. Lightly cover and leave
to stand in a cool place, but not the refrigerator, for
30 minutes to let the flavours develop. Stir again
and serve with chicken or fish kebabs.

asian peach salsa

ingredients

makes about 400 g/
14 oz

3 ripe peaches
1–2 bird's eye chillies
2 lemon grass stalks
2.5-cm/1-inch piece fresh
    ginger
2 tsp sesame oil
1 whole star anise
2 tsp soy sauce
1 tbsp clear honey
1 small pak choi, about
    25 g/1 oz, finely shredded
1 tbsp sesame seeds

method

1 Make a cross in the top of each peach, put in a large heatproof bowl and pour over boiling water to cover. Leave to stand for 1–2 minutes, then remove with a slotted spoon and leave to cool. When cool enough to handle, peel away the skins. Cut in half, remove and discard the stones and finely chop the flesh.

2 Cut the chilli in half, remove and discard the seeds and membrane and finely chop. Remove and discard the outer leaves of the lemon grass stalks and lightly bruise with a mallet or rolling pin. Cut into small pieces. Peel the ginger and finely grate.

3 Heat a wok for 30 seconds over a high heat. Add the oil, swirl around to coat the bottom of the wok and heat for 30 seconds. Add the chilli, ginger, lemon grass and star anise and stir-fry for 1 minute. Add the peaches with the soy sauce, honey and pak choi and stir-fry for 2 minutes. Spoon the salsa into a bowl.

4 Lightly cover and leave to stand in a cool place, but not the refrigerator, for 30 minutes to let the flavours develop. Carefully remove the lemon grass pieces and star anise. Sprinkle with the sesame seeds and serve.

turkish salsa

ingredients

makes about 500 g/
1 lb 2 oz

1–2 (or to taste) fresh red
    jalapeño chillies
4 spring onions, finely chopped
2 oranges
1 ripe pomegranate
2 ripe figs
2 tsp clear honey
1 tbsp snipped fresh chives
1 tsp toasted cumin seeds
pitta bread, to serve

method

1 Cut the chillies in half, remove and discard the seeds
   and membrane and finely chop. Put in a bowl with the
   spring onions.

2 Working over the bowl to catch the juices, peel the
   oranges, removing and discarding all the bitter white
   pith. Separate into segments, finely chop the flesh and
   add to the chillies and spring onions.

3 Cut the pomegranate in half and scoop out the seeds.
   Add them to the orange mixture. Lightly rinse the figs
   and finely chop.

4 Add the chopped figs to the bowl with the honey and
   chives. Stir well and spoon into a non-metallic serving
   dish. Lightly cover and leave to stand in a cool place,
   but not the refrigerator, for 30 minutes to let the
   flavours develop. Sprinkle with the cumin seeds
   and serve with pitta bread.

jamaican salsa

ingredients

*makes about 600 g/
1 lb 5 oz*

25 g/1 oz drained canned
    sweetcorn
1 large ripe banana
finely grated rind of 1 lime
2 tbsp freshly squeezed
    lime juice
2 ripe guavas, about 115 g/4 oz
    total weight
1–2 fresh Jamaican hot chillies,
    deseeded and finely chopped
1 small red onion, finely chopped
1 tsp (or to taste) clear honey
300 ml/10 fl oz plain yogurt
1 tbsp chopped fresh coriander,
    plus extra to garnish
pepper
barbecued chicken, to serve

method

1 Cook the sweetcorn in a saucepan of boiling water for
    3–4 minutes until tender. Drain well.

2 Peel the banana and mash it in a non-metallic bowl.
    Add the lime rind and juice, then gently stir until the
    banana is thoroughly coated in the lime juice. Stir in
    the sweetcorn.

3 Peel the guavas, deseed and finely chop the flesh.
    Add to the bowl with the chilli, onion and honey.

4 Stir in the yogurt with the coriander and pepper to
    taste. Stir well, then spoon into a serving bowl. Lightly
    cover and leave to stand in a cool place, but not the
    refrigerator, for at least 30 minutes to let all the flavours
    develop. Garnish with fresh coriander and serve with
    barbecued chicken.

yogurt salsa

ingredients

makes about 500 g/
1 lb 2 oz

7.5-cm/3-inch piece cucumber
1 tsp salt
4 spring onions, finely chopped
1 courgette, grated
1 red pepper, deseeded
    and finely chopped
300 ml/10 fl oz Greek-style
    yogurt
1 tbsp chopped fresh
    flat-leaf parsley
1–2 tsp (or to taste) chilli
    powder
pepper
lamb kebabs, to serve

method

1 Cut the cucumber lengthways into quarters. Scoop out and discard the seeds. Coarsely grate the flesh, put in a non-metallic sieve and sprinkle with the salt. Leave to drain for 15–20 minutes, then rinse thoroughly and drain well. Put in a small bowl.

2 Add the spring onions, courgette and red pepper to the bowl and mix well. Add the yogurt and parsley with the chilli powder and pepper to taste. Stir well, then spoon into a serving dish. Lightly cover and leave to stand in a cool place, but not the refrigerator, for at least 30 minutes to let the flavours develop. Serve with lamb kebabs.

low-fat yogurt salsa

ingredients

*makes about 375 g/
13 oz*

55 g/2 oz ready-to-eat dried
    apricots
300 ml/10 fl oz low-fat Greek-style
    or natural yogurt
3 tbsp rolled oats
1–2 tsp (or to taste) clear honey
1 fresh green jalapeño chilli,
    deseeded and finely chopped
6 spring onions, finely chopped
1 carrot, about 115 g/4 oz,
    peeled and grated
2 tbsp chopped fresh mint
few dashes of hot pepper sauce,
    to taste
pepper
cooked corn cobs, to serve

method

1 Finely chop the apricots and put in a small bowl. Add the yogurt with the rolled oats and honey.

2 Stir well, then add the chilli, spring onions, carrot and mint with pepper to taste. Stir again, then add the hot pepper sauce.

3 Spoon into a serving bowl. Lightly cover and leave to stand in a cool place, but not the refrigerator, for at least 30 minutes to let the flavours develop. Store in the refrigerator if keeping for longer. Serve with cooked corn cobs.

herb salsa

ingredients

makes about 350 g/12 oz

7.5-cm/3-inch piece cucumber
2 tsp salt
6 spring onions, finely chopped
2 celery sticks, finely chopped
1 green pepper, peeled, deseeded
    and finely chopped
150 ml/5 fl oz low-fat Greek-style
    or natural yogurt
1 tbsp shredded fresh basil
1 tbsp chopped fresh
    flat-leaf parsley
1 tbsp chopped fresh oregano
grilled salmon steaks,
    to serve

method

1 Peel the cucumber very thinly and cut lengthways into quarters. Scoop out and discard the seeds. Finely chop the flesh, put in a non-metallic sieve and sprinkle with the salt. Leave to drain for 15–20 minutes, then rinse thoroughly and drain well. Put in a small bowl.

2 Add the spring onions, celery and green pepper to the bowl and mix well. Add the yogurt and stir well before adding all the herbs. Stir again, then spoon into a serving dish. Lightly cover and leave to stand in a cool place, but not the refrigerator, for 30 minutes to let the flavours develop. Serve with grilled salmon steaks.

sweet
sauces

french chocolate sauce

ingredients

makes about 150 ml/
5 fl oz

90 ml/3 fl oz double cream
85 g/3 oz plain chocolate,
     broken into small pieces
2 tbsp orange liqueur

method

1 Bring the cream gently to the boil in a small heavy-based saucepan over a low heat. Remove the pan from the heat, add the broken chocolate and stir until smooth.

2 Stir in the liqueur and serve immediately, or keep the sauce warm until required.

chocolate brandy sauce

ingredients

makes about 300 ml/
10 fl oz

250 g/9 oz plain chocolate, broken
   into pieces (must contain at
   least 50 per cent cocoa solids)
100 ml/3½ fl oz double cream
2 tbsp brandy

method

1 Place the chocolate into the top of a double boiler
   or in a heatproof bowl set over a saucepan of
   simmering water.

2 Pour in the cream and stir until the chocolate is
   melted and smooth. Stir in the brandy, pour into a jug
   and serve.

white chocolate fudge sauce

ingredients

makes about 350 ml/
12 fl oz

150 ml/5 fl oz double cream
4 tbsp unsalted butter, cut into
    small pieces
3 tbsp caster sugar
175 g/6 oz white chocolate,
    broken into pieces
2 tbsp brandy

method

1 Pour the cream into the top of a double boiler or
   a heatproof bowl set over a saucepan of gently
   simmering water. Add the butter and sugar and stir
   until the mixture is smooth. Remove from the heat.

2 Stir in the chocolate, a few pieces at a time, waiting for
   the chocolate to melt before adding the next. Add the
   brandy and stir the sauce until smooth. Cool to room
   temperature before serving.

mocha sauce

ingredients

makes about 425 ml/
15 fl oz

150 ml/5 fl oz double cream
115 g/4 oz unsalted butter
55 g/2 oz soft light brown sugar
175 g/6 oz plain chocolate,
    broken into pieces
1 tbsp instant coffee granules
2 tbsp dark rum (optional)

method

1 Pour the cream into a heatproof bowl and add the butter and sugar. Set over a saucepan of gently simmering water and cook, stirring constantly, until smooth. Remove the sauce from the heat and set aside to cool slightly.

2 Stir in the chocolate and coffee granules and continue stirring until the chocolate has melted and the coffee dissolved. Stir in the rum, if using, then leave the sauce to cool to room temperature before serving.

vanilla toffee sauce

ingredients

makes about 700 ml/
1¼ pints

125 g/4½ oz butter
400 g/14 oz soft light brown sugar
225 ml/8 fl oz golden syrup
2 tbsp maple syrup
2 tbsp water
400 ml/14 fl oz canned
    condensed milk
1 tsp vanilla extract
½ tsp ground cinnamon
1 tbsp rum

method

1 Put the butter into a heatproof bowl set over a saucepan of simmering water and melt gently. Add the sugar, golden syrup, maple syrup, water, condensed milk, vanilla extract and cinnamon.

2 Stir until thick and smooth, then stir in the rum and cook for another minute. Remove from the heat and carefully pour the mixture into a jug and serve.

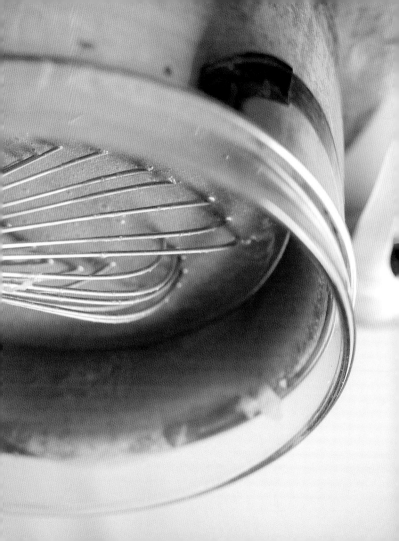

nutty butterscotch sauce

ingredients

makes about 300 ml/
10 fl oz

350 g/12 oz soft light brown sugar
125 ml/4 fl oz water
1 tbsp rum
85 g/3 oz unsalted butter
125 ml/4 fl oz double cream,
    gently warmed
85 g/3 oz peanuts, chopped

method

1 Put the sugar and water into a heavy-based saucepan, place over a medium heat and stir until the sugar has dissolved. Bring to the boil, then leave the sauce to bubble for 6–7 minutes. Stir in the rum and cook for another minute.

2 Remove from the heat and carefully stir in the butter until melted. Gradually stir in the cream until the mixture is smooth. Finally, stir in the nuts and serve.

maple sauce

ingredients

makes about 175 ml/
6 fl oz

175 ml/6 fl oz maple syrup
4 tbsp butter
½ tsp ground mixed spice

method

1 Put all the ingredients into a saucepan over a medium heat. Bring to the boil, stirring, then reduce the heat and simmer for 3 minutes.

2 Remove from the heat, carefully pour the mixture into a jar, and serve warm or cold.

custard sauce

ingredients

makes about 600 ml/
1 pint

25 g/1 oz cornflour
600 ml/1 pint milk
55 g/2 oz sugar
25 g/1 oz unsalted butter
1 egg
½ tsp vanilla extract

method

1 Put the cornflour into a bowl with 3 tablespoons of the milk. Stir to a paste. Put the remaining milk in a saucepan and bring just to the boil.

2 Meanwhile, put the sugar, butter, egg and vanilla extract into a food processor and process until smooth.

3 Pour the hot milk into the cornflour mixture, stirring constantly. Return to the pan and cook over a low heat, stirring constantly, for 2 minutes or until thick. With the motor running, pour the hot cornflour mixture into the food processor and process until well combined with the sugar mixture. Pour the custard into a jug and serve immediately.

variation

Stir in 1 tablespoon of liqueur, such as rum or cognac, while the custard is in the food processor, or just before serving.

berry sauce

ingredients

makes about 225 ml/
8 fl oz

225 g/8 oz berries, such as
   blackberries or raspberries
2 tbsp water
2–3 tbsp caster sugar
2 tbsp fruit liqueur, such as crème
   de cassis or crème de framboise

method

1 Put all the ingredients into a small, heavy-based
   saucepan and heat gently, until the sugar has dissolved
   and the fruit juices run.

2 Purée the ingredients in a food processor, then push
   through a non-metallic sieve into a serving bowl to
   remove the seeds. Add more sugar if necessary and
   serve warm or cold.

orange sauce

ingredients

makes about 125 ml/
4 fl oz

55 g/2 oz caster sugar
1 tbsp water
finely grated rind of 1 large orange
125 ml/4 fl oz freshly squeezed
    orange juice
55 g/2 oz unsalted butter, diced
1 tbsp orange liqueur

method

1 Place the sugar in a wide sauté pan or frying pan over
  a medium heat and stir in the water. Continue stirring
  until the sugar dissolves, then increase the heat to high
  and leave the syrup to bubble for 1–2 minutes until it
  just begins to turn golden brown.

2 Stir in the orange rind and juice, then add the butter
  and continue stirring until it melts. Stir in the orange
  liqueur, remove from the heat and serve warm.

peach coulis

ingredients

makes about 300 ml/
10 fl oz

450 g/1 lb peaches
1 tbsp lemon juice
2 tbsp caster sugar
2 tbsp amaretto liqueur

method

1 Using a sharp knife, cut a cross in the base of each peach, then plunge into boiling water for 15–30 seconds. Drain and refresh in iced water. Peel off the skins, halve the peaches and remove the stones, then slice coarsely.

2 Put the peaches, lemon juice and sugar into a food processor. Process to a smooth purée, scraping down the sides as necessary. Transfer to a bowl and stir in the liqueur. Cover and chill for 1 hour before serving.

fruit coulis

ingredients

*makes about 300 ml/
10 fl oz each*

melba coulis
450 g/1 lb raspberries
1 tbsp lemon juice
3 tbsp caster sugar

tropical fruits coulis
1 mango
1 papaya
3 kiwi fruit
2 tbsp caster sugar
3 tbsp white rum

method

1 For the melba coulis, put the fruit, lemon juice and
sugar into a food processor. Process to a smooth paste,
scraping down the sides as necessary, then push
through a non-metallic sieve into a bowl to remove
the seeds. Cover and chill in the refrigerator for 1 hour
before serving.

2 For the tropical fruits coulis, stone the mango and
put the flesh into a food processor. Cut the papaya
in half lengthways and scoop out the seeds with a
spoon. Scoop out any fibres. Discard the seeds and
fibres. Scoop out the flesh, chop coarsely and add to
the food processor. Slice the kiwi fruit and add to the
food processor with the sugar.

3 Process to a purée, scraping down the sides as
necessary, then push through a non-metallic sieve
into a bowl. Stir in the rum. Cover and chill for 1 hour
before serving.

index

anchovy
  spinach & anchovy sauce
    88
apple
  apple & habanero chilli
    salsa 160
  apple sauce 34
arrabbiata sauce 60
Asian peach salsa 170
asparagus sauce 22
aubergine
  fragrant aubergine sauce
    112
avocado salsa 152

bacon
  tomato, mushroom &
    bacon sauce 72
barbecue sauce 54
basil
  basil, chive & lemon
    dressing 128
  basil pesto 28
Béarnaise sauce 10
Béchamel sauce 8
berry sauce 200
beurre blanc 16
blue cheese & broccoli
  sauce 104
Bolognese sauce 66
bread sauce 18
bucatini with lamb & yellow
  pepper sauce 70
buttered pea & cheese
  sauce 106
butternut squash
  creamy butternut squash
    sauce 102

carbonara sauce 74
Caribbean salsa 164
cheese
  blue cheese & broccoli
    sauce 104
  buttered pea & cheese
    sauce 106
  creamy cheese sauce 94
  gorgonzola sauce 98
  ricotta sauce 96
chicken
  creamy chicken sauce 78
chilli
  apple & habanero chilli
    salsa 160
  chilli & garlic salsa 162
  chilli sauce 48

garlic, chilli & oregano oil
    126
chipotle sauce 52
chocolate
  chocolate brandy sauce
    186
  French chocolate sauce
    184
  mocha sauce 190
  white chocolate fudge
    sauce 188
corn
  roasted corn salsa 154
courgette
  hot courgette sauce 110
crab
  spicy crab sauce 82
cranberry sauce 36
creamy butternut squash
  sauce 102
creamy cheese sauce 94
creamy chicken sauce 78
creamy mushroom
  sauce 100
Creole pineapple salsa 166
custard sauce 198

dill & peppercorn vinegar
  124

fennel
  sardine & fennel sauce 86
fragrant aubergine
  sauce 112
French chocolate sauce 184
fresh tomato sauce 56
fruit coulis 206

garlic
  chilli & garlic salsa 162
  garlic, chilli & oregano
    oil 126
  garlic vinaigrette 120
  garlic walnut sauce 114
  roasted pepper & garlic
    dressing 130
gorgonzola sauce 98
gravy 38
green dressing 132
green vegetable sauce 108

herb
  herb salsa 180
  herb vinaigrette 122
  olive oil & herb sauce 116
hollandaise sauce 12

honey & yogurt
  dressing 140
horseradish sauce 24
hot courgette sauce 110

Jamaican salsa 174

lamb
  bucatini with lamb &
    yellow pepper sauce
    70
low-fat yogurt salsa 178

maple sauce 196
Mediterranean sauce 64
melba coulis 206
Mexican salsa 156
mild horseradish sauce 24
mint sauce 26
mocha sauce 190
mole sauce 50
mushroom
  creamy mushroom sauce
    100
  tomato, mushroom &
    bacon sauce 72
mussel
  saffron mussel sauce 84

nutty butterscotch
  sauce 194

olive oil & herb sauce 116
orange sauce 202

parsley sauce 20
pea
  buttered pea & cheese
    sauce 106
peach
  Asian peach salsa 170
  peach coulis 204
pepper
  bucatini with lamb &
    yellow pepper sauce
    70
  roasted pepper & garlic
    dressing 130
pineapple
  Creole pineapple salsa
    166
pink grapefruit, raspberry,
  wasabi & sesame oil
  dressing 142
pumpkin sauce with Parma
  ham 76

red wine sauce 40
ricotta sauce 96
roasted corn salsa 154
roasted pepper & garlic
  dressing 130

saffron mussel sauce 84
sardine & fennel sauce 86
satay sauce 44
seafood sauce 80
slim-line dressing 134
smoked salmon
  smoked salmon &
    watercress sauce 90
  smoked salmon cream
    sauce 92
spicy crab sauce 82
spinach & anchovy sauce 88
sweet & sour
  sweet & sour dressing
    138
  sweet & sour sauce 46

tapenade 32
tarragon meatball sauce 68
teriyaki sauce 42
tex-mex salsa 158
three bean salsa 150
tomatillo
  warm tomatillo salsa 148
tomato
  fresh tomato sauce 56
  sun-dried tomato pesto
    30
  sun-dried tomato sauce
    62
  tomato dressing 136
  tomato, mushroom &
    bacon sauce 72
  tomato salsa 146
tropical fruits coulis 206
tropical salsa 168
Turkish salsa 172

vanilla toffee sauce 192
velouté sauce 14

warm tomatillo salsa 148
watercress
  watercress & smoked
    salmon sauce 90

yogurt
  honey & yogurt dressing
    140
  low-fat yogurt salsa 178
  yogurt salsa 176